What's in the Panties?

Understanding the psyche of a woman one panty at a time

Dr. Marlena Corcoran

"What's sexy and charming and an essential part of every day? Getting dressed! Or not!! Cheryl L. Smith's endearing ode to the communications code of women's panties provides long-term lovers with an endlessly entertaining, seriously flirtatious way to keep an endearing form of curiosity alive. Through the story of a couple and their friends and organized into chapters featuring different styles, 'What's in the Panties?' keeps us looking for more–or less, as the case may be."

Peter Thomas

"Cheryl, all I can say is "Thank You!" I finally understand the method behind the Panty madness! It almost all makes sense now :) I really enjoyed the way this was written. It takes you through a story and backs it with data of intriguing facts that back up each segment of the story and done in a way that makes it hard to put this book down! Very enjoyable read!!"

Elizabeth (Liz) Lim

"A seemingly light-hearted look at ladies undergarments that really is a book about improving communication in your marriage. Cheryl entices us into a young couples exploration of fashion in doing so teaches us how we can be more loving and caring with each other. A fun read that will give any couple new insights into each other!!"

Barry Watson

'This author has zero hesitation in going where few have gone before. She addresses a topic that people of both sexes think about more than they probably admit - women's panties. Rather than a sleazy approach, she tackles this topic with humor, history and heartfelt passion. I had absolutely no idea there was so much to learn about such a small piece of fabric! This book will inform you, enlighten you and cause you to smile at the home truths we all face around the fascinating topic of women's panties."

Dan Friberg

"'What's in the Panties?' is amazing! I had never thought about panties that way before! The author brought a whole new realization to me as to how women approach this, and how men should learn a lesson as well! Well done!"

Violette Roberts

"Clever and well written! Great historical tidbits and anecdotes from a woman's point of view, which also appeal to a man's sensibilities just as easily. Uplifting, humorous, insightful - can't wait for Cheryl's next book!"

As a way to say "thank you" for your interest in my book, here is my gift to you.

http://www.subscribepage.com/PowerOfHappiness

What's In the Panties?

What's In the Panties?

Understanding the psyche of a
woman`one panty at a time

Cheryl L. Smith

To my mom, my hero, my friend. There are no words to describe the gift that God gave me when you became my mom.

Table of Contents

Introduction

Have you ever really thought about panties? No, not like *that*. I'm talking about the curiosity as to the intrigue they've inspired for centuries. Have you ever wondered, when the subject is simply mentioned among friends or with a significant other, Why so much excitement? Maybe you've never given the topic the time of day—or maybe you're like me, secretly wondering but never really taking the time to explore the allure "behind the panties."

Panties have carried with them a sense of wonderment and enticement simply due to their hidden value (*hidden*, that is, underneath the clothes). From young boys wanting to see a girl in a pair of panties to the millions of dollars spent on lingerie for the "big reveal" on wedding night (or for spicing up a dry marriage years later) or to a girl just simply wanting to feel special in her favorite pair of panties. It is true that in one way or another panties have been a huge part of every person's life—both men and women.

Well, the secret is about to be uncovered. No more guessing. No more contemplating the "why." No more hush-hush, cloak-and-dagger, coded messages.

I'm finally about to blow the lid on that age-old mystery: "What's in the panties?"

As a woman myself, and someone who has had her fair share of panty styles, I wanted to understand the "why." I wanted to know if there was more to this panty thing than meets the eye. So I started the research. I spoke with marketing agencies, women young and old, specialty stores and even men. I conducted surveys, asked women about their panty selections while they were shopping for that special pair. I was a woman on a mission and I was a woman who wanted answers.

Let's face it. Women—and men, too—are spending millions of dollars on panties each year, from holiday to holiday and every day in between. The advertising dollars put into this market are astronomical and we as consumers take the bait. So what is it? What is the attraction? The color? The season? The style? The mood?

This book will answer every question you've ever had about the subject. It will not only give you insight into the various types of panties but it will speak to the reasons why specific panty choices are made. I will address the emotional aspects of panty selection, and there may even be some hidden gems that will teach you how to choose panties to redirect attitudes, moods and paths of success.

As crazy as this may all seem, panties do indeed play a more significant role in our lives than we may have ever thought possible. When a woman puts on a carefully selected panty for the day, one that makes her feel comfortable and speaks to her whole self, it's as though she's gearing up in her superhero outfit.

During my research, Courtney Roberts, one of the individuals who excitedly participated in my "What's in the Panties?" survey, had this to say: "Any time I have a new pair of panties on, the possibilities of life seem endless!"

What a testimony to the power of the panties! So maybe it is true. Maybe there is more to "the panty thing" than we've given it credit all of these years.

I promise that you will see panties in a whole new light after reading this book. Women, you will understand the decisions you make during the panty selection; you will discover newfound opportunities to potentially change your path and meet each new challenge with a smile. And men—I promise you will know exactly what and what not to expect when certain panties are worn. You will have a deeper understanding of the symbolic value of your lady's panty choice; you may even discover some ideas for changing her mood for the day.

Whether man or woman, by understanding "what's in the panties," we can create an outcome you can both enjoy.

But don't wait. New journeys await as you venture down this panty path. There are many hidden gems within these pages—and some jewels! And they are just a panty away.

Treat yourself to some fun, some introspection, some learning and of course some panties as you read through the following pages. A topic not widely discussed is sure to bring a smile on your face and knowledge for years to come.

Panties 101

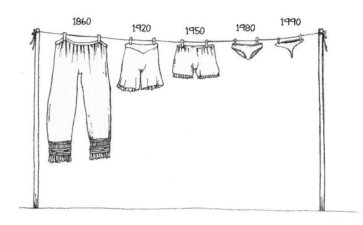

"You can tell a lot about a person from their underwear." ~ *Rachael Bilson*

Have you ever noticed that clothing, electronics, cookware, cars and the way we do business as a whole always change over the years? We like to say that these changes make us more efficient. We are futuristic in our thinking, growing our minds and our resources for the good of all people. This is true, to a point, but the real underlying reason behind this is the desire for *more*. We don't always know what "more" will look like, but we constantly crave it.

Panties certainly have their place in that school of thought as well.

Let's look at electronics for a moment. At one point we had the VCR as a device to watch our most sought-after movies. It was big, cumbersome and clunky in its appearance and in its functionality. However, we loved it and felt it had revolutionized the in-home viewing experience. And, for that time period, we could all agree with that statement.

Now let's jump over to panties (we'll come back to the VCR in a moment). In 1949, Gertude "Gussie" Moran, an American tennis player, caused a huge uproar while becoming an overnight sensation when she decided to challenge the Wimbledon dress code. She had become tired of the stale, simple tennis outfits that were considered "appropriate" by the American Tennis Association and decided to take matters into her own hands by adding some flair to her style.

So what did she do? She added lace around the edges of the leg openings of her bottoms. Today we would think nothing of this, but in 1949 it was a big, international story. It was unheard of to see such daring and risqué attire in a public setting. Nonetheless, the photographers were there to catch those "panty shots." It was all over the news. Previously, Gussie had only been known to be "just an average girl," according to the press, but once those lacy bottoms hit the wire, she had become an overnight starlet and was soon known as "Gorgeous Gussie."

Oddly enough, tennis players today like Serena Williams have also brought heightened visibility to underwear through the utilization of "boy shorts," which others may refer to as "booty shorts," as part of their regular tennis attire. The need for underwear has never changed, but how they are worn and for what purpose has always evolved.

Going back to the VCR: as time went on, technology advanced and the need for something new, smaller, slicker and, yes, sexier came about. The DVD was introduced. Everyone loved it. It had all the consumer wanted and then some. And when *that* wasn't enough, when we wanted still *more*, the Blu-ray came into the picture and we willingly paid top dollar for these advancements. Sound familiar? Absolutely. As consumers, we always take the bait. Whether in the world of technology or in the latest seductive trends of panty fashion, we live in a state of expectation, dreaming of a product that will far exceed anything we could ever imagine.

To this end, if we look at the timeline of underwear, we see that the same is true. We started with modest undergarments and advanced to the edgy styles of today. And why? We wanted something more alluring, more provocative and, yes, more sexy, just like the DVD player. Our appetite for "more" was never satisfied, and still isn't today, which is why advancements will continue to occur in every niche known to humankind.

Although we see how trends change from generation to generation, we also see how history tends to repeat itself. Have you ever heard someone say, "Don't get rid of those pants. Wait twenty years and they'll be back in style"? Believe it or not, in some aspects of the transformation of underwear, we have turned back time.

During the Victorian era (1837–1901), women wore knickers. These articles of clothing were worn with the entire crotch area left open and exposed because it was believed to be more hygienic and the change of underwear was less frequent than today. Therefore, it was felt that women should not have anything between their legs. Today, women spend top dollar on crotchless panties for those "special nights." Yes, a far different purpose, but still—a style has returned.

Furthermore, in the nineteenth century, women wore large, heavy petticoats because it was considered "unladylike" to wear underwear underneath. Of course, eventually bloomers and knickers came on the scene, but at the onset, going "commando" was the norm for ladies of that era. Today, approximately 15% of women admit that going "commando" is an option for them depending on how they feel and the style of clothing they're wearing.

Over the course of many years, women began to change what was considered appropriate in the world of attire and began to venture into unchartered territory. In this, panties too began to see an overhaul. Women were becoming more free in their decisions and opinions. In fact, men were quite pleased with the changes in the undergarment industry. After all, they greatly benefited from the sexy styles being thrown their way and were all too eager to show their approval.

The bikini era was certainly one of intrigue, one that fought an uphill battle to gain approval and acceptance in the undergarment market. We can thank French engineer Louis Reard, who in 1949 created the bikini swimsuit, naming it after Bikini Atoll, an island in the Pacific Ocean. The bikini was not allowed to be worn in many places, however, and women who wore it were told they had no common decency and no tact. Nonetheless, for most women, wearing a bikini swimsuit was a form of a second liberation. It was a way to embrace freedom and not focus on sexuality.

Although there was much controversy, over time famous movie stars took to the big screen wearing bikinis in various beach scenes, ultimately paving the way for mass acceptance of the style. By the 1960s, bikini underwear started to evolve from thongs to french cut and low-rise styles. Today, bikini underwear is routinely worn in blockbuster hits, media advertisements and of course by women in everyday life.

Surprisingly, G-strings and thongs entered the picture almost a hundred years ago, during the 1920s when they were first worn by showgirls. Exotic and go-go dancers made these skivvies popular because most showrooms did not want completely nude dancers; the use of the G-string under short, provocative costumes was just enough to keep the gentlemen customers entertained. By the 1980s and into the 1990s, the G-string and the thong—and all the variations of each—became quite popular among women in the Western world, and even advanced to be regularly worn as a swimsuit bottom.

So where does this history find us today? How do women now feel about their panties? Is there really still a sense of liberation experienced when a woman puts on a new pair of panties? Let's face it. Panties are now widely accepted among all types of people through advertisements, store displays and open discussion. So does that open the views and the attitudes people have about the dark secrets of panty mystique? Does a woman embrace a feeling of power through the acceptance of herself and to the world through the ability to *choose* the panty styles she will wear from day to day? Does she feel empowered, ready to conquer any challenge with the panty options that have been presented to her?

I wanted to know the answers to these questions. I knew how I felt and loved having options, often finding myself selecting certain panties for certain occasions. Whether a date night, a family gathering or a "big shot" meeting, I had a pair of panties that would invoke a particular feeling of self assuredness that would be my partner, if you will, through the occasion. It was like having my own little superpower in my panties.

Because I recognized this in myself, I wanted to know what other women were thinking, and I really wanted to know if a woman, someone like me, could communicate her thoughts, change her attitude for the day and even redirect her life in some form or fashion through her choice of panties and the way she feels in them.

So I asked, and women responded.

Here is what the ladies had to say.
(The answers below represent the most popular responses for each question.)

1. What is the determining factor in your daily panty selection?
   Types of clothing: 38%
   Comfort: 27%

2. What are your favorite types of panties?
   Bikini: 30%
   Booty Shorts: 24%
   Thong: 23%
   Granny Panties: 13%

3. Do you own period panties?
   Yes: 70%

4. What is your favorite color of panties?
   Black: 55%
   Pink: 12%

> *"You don't buy black lingerie unless you want someone to see it."*
> *–from the movie* 10 Things I Hate About You

5. How do your favorite panties make you feel?
Sexy: 34%
Relaxed: 23%
Confident: 21%

These next four questions are those that will most help us understand the psyche of a woman through her panty choices.

6. Does a woman's panty selection determine how a woman will go about her day?
Yes: 65%

7. Can a woman express her feelings and mood to her boyfriend or husband through the type of panties she's wearing?
Yes: 95%

8. Do you feel that wearing certain styles of panties can make you feel more confident, bold, happy, sexy, fun, sad, boring, etc.?
Yes: 84%

9. Do you feel that changing your style of panty selection can change the way you carry yourself and lead to more overall success in your life?
Yes: 75%

With this data, it can be said that panties do in fact have an impact on the lives of women, and their daily choices can also affect their professional and personal lives. Consequently, this information can be used by men to better understand their wives or girlfriends. Women can learn to shape their life by understanding the value of specific types, colors and styles of panties.

Of course, this new way of thinking will take some work. Nothing worth having is easy and if you're looking to grow, learn and reach new heights of success in your life at any and all levels, then put in the work. The rewards will be great!

In the following pages, I will introduce you to Trevor and Whitney, a married couple whose lives are about to be changed through their own, unique panty journey. They have no idea as to the road that lies ahead, but surely the rewards will be great. Each chapter will introduce a different style of panties as Trevor is awakened to the hidden gem of *What's in the Panties?* Through this enlightenment, he will learn how to shape his relationship around the knowledge he has acquired and grow a stronger, more fulfilling marriage with Whitney. Whitney will learn more about herself through the types of panties she chooses to wear each day.

Just as panties have evolved over the years, I hope you too will allow your thoughts and preconceived notions of panties to evolve and to find your own hidden treasure of *What's in the Panties?*

Bikini Day

The alarm clock rang just as Trevor had turned over to snuggle with his adorable wife, Whitney. They were both tired and fighting the Monday morning blues. The weekend had been long—running from store to store, paying bills and taking time to visit Whitney's parents, not to mention going to the dog park with Digger (named, appropriately, after the many holes left in the backyard). The visit with Whitney's parents always made for a long day, as Mrs. Griffith loved to cook, while telling stories of generations past and ending the night with a good movie. And now the weekend was gone and the work week was starting.

The alarm still rang. Trevor kept hitting the snooze button in between momentary naps.

"Do you think we can ask for the day off?" Whitney asked in between yawns. "We haven't really taken any vacation time other than your family reunion." That had been a few months back.

"I guess we could," said Trevor. "What could it hurt? Then we could take some time for ourselves and just hang out and do some of the things we've been talking about doing around the house."

"Sounds like a plan to me," said Whitney.

Whitney and Trevor both had high demanding jobs. Trevor was a Technical Consultant for Inlite, a multimedia company with high-end clients, while Whitney worked in the fashion industry directly supporting the CEO of Tribe Designs. They had worked hard to get to these positions and money was good. They were still young, with no kids, and had just celebrated their fourth year of marriage. Life seemed to always smile down upon them and for all outward appearances, they had no problems. However, like every couple, they experienced their own share of problems. These somehow always seemed to stem from a lack of communication in one way or another.

The two continued to catch some sleep for another hour or so before getting up to call in to their jobs. Without any problem, the two received the green light from their bosses and started making plans for the day. With excitement and a sense of freedom, they headed toward the kitchen, Trevor in his navy blue boxers and Whitney in a short, light yellow nightie.

"I think I'm going to have some bacon and eggs," said Trevor.

"Sounds good. I'll make the coffee," Whitney chimed in.

"I know we had talked about cleaning out some of those boxes in the garage. Do you feel up to that today, or would you rather wait another day?" asked Trevor.

"Sure. That's fine." Whitney seemed a bit irritated at the thought.

Trevor already knew what the "that's fine" statement really meant. It was more about her just going along with the flow rather than it being something she really wanted to do. So he asked again.

"Are you sure, babe? We can wait another day if you'd like."

"Yes. I said it's fine." Her tone was a little less abrasive the second time around. She added, "Then, when we're done, I thought we'd go down to the beach and take in some sun. Get cooled off. It's so hot right now. I'm sure the water is great."

Although it sounded like fun, Trevor thought it a bit odd. Whitney was usually the one wanting to take advantage of every spare minute of a day off with cleaning, organizing or some other type of chore. Nonetheless, Trevor was certainly going to be grateful for this change of pace. He too could enjoy some time at the beach. The summer had been very warm and would continue that way over the next few weeks at least.

The two of them prepared breakfast together and playfully interacted in the kitchen, almost like newlyweds again. They were definitely going to enjoy this day off and make the most of it. Sometimes, alone time without the pressures of work and family could make all the difference in the world.

After throwing on some old clothes, Trevor and Whitney made their way to the garage. There were definitely more boxes than either one of them had remembered, but they could go through them quickly with both of them working together. Box by box, they chose what to keep and what to throw away. They laughed at some of the items, like Whitney's old cheerleading outfit from high school and Trevor's Boy Scout vest covered in badges. They were enjoying this walk down memory lane, making fun of one another as they sorted through their prized possessions.

"Are you really going to keep that, Trevor?" Whitney asked. "I mean, why is that old race car set so important? It doesn't even run and it's just taking up space."

"I'll have you know this race car set looks so old and worn because it is. It was given to my dad by my grandfather. Now it's been passed down to me," Trevor explained. "It's very special."

Whitney just sat quietly listening to the story. She realized that deep down inside, Trevor really was a sentimental and caring man, in spite of the tough demeanor he often carried to get through his work day.

As they continued making their way through the "war of the boxes," Trevor began laughing.

"What are these?" he asked.

"Give me those," Whitney yelled. "Those are mine."

"And these, too?" Trevor added, still snickering.

"Oh, my goodness. Give me that box. I can't believe I still have these—all of these ..."

One by one, panty by panty, Whitney pulled from the box countless panties that she'd had from high school and college. Pink ones, blue ones, lacy ones and satin ones.

There were some thongs, some granny panties and, of course, her beloved bikinis. When she came across what she remembered had been her favorite pair, she just stared and smiled. There, in her hand, was a lavender pair of bikinis with a tiny bow right at the front. Nothing special, but a pair she had absolutely loved.

"I used to wear these when I was in college. They were just comfortable and I always felt free and relaxed. Nothing seemed to bother me. Whether I was hanging out with my friends or getting ready to see my special honey," she looked over to Trevor and met him with a sweet kiss, "these panties were my 'everything' pair."

Trevor really didn't know what to say. He was lost. He had never heard anyone speak so fondly of some ... panties? But he definitely took notice and realized how Whitney's whole tone and mood seemed to instantly soften. It was actually pretty amazing.

As they finished up the garage and put everything back in its place, they headed back in the house to get ready for the beach.

"Did you keep out that box of panties, babe?" asked Trevor.

"No," said Whitney. "But I know where they are."

"You should bring them in the house."

Whitney was a bit surprised at this. Truly, the box was just filled with different panties that she'd grown to love over the years and for some odd reason had kept. She didn't expect Trevor to understand this. Nonetheless, she excitedly grabbed the box and took it inside.

As the two of them showered and began getting ready for their afternoon rendezvous, Trevor asked about the bikinis.

"Why don't you wear those lavender pair of panties you found in the garage earlier?"

"The bikinis?" Whitney asked.

"Yeah, I guess that's what they're called," he said, and they both chuckled.

"OK, great! But you know they're not as new and pretty as some of the others I have in my drawer."

"It doesn't matter," he said. "I just want to see you in them."

Trevor stood and watched his beautiful wife slip into the aged yet still attractive lavender bikinis. They were simple, but oh how his wife loved them, which in turn put a smile on his face. She was gorgeous. She was sexy. It didn't even matter at that moment what she had on—she was thrilled and Trevor could see what a change a simple pair of panties could have on a woman.

Whitney finished getting ready and then it was time to go.

"You know, babe, you should wear those panties whenever you want to. I love seeing you in anything, just so you know, but seeing you today and seeing how much you loved those little bikinis showed me something too."

"What's that, Trevor?" she asked.

"What's in the panties is really not all about looking good for the man. It's just as much about the woman and how she feels in them."

Whitney smiled and nodded in agreement, and off to the beach they went. Tomorrow would be another day back at work, so they were going to enjoy this day–this Bikini Day.

* * *

"I just threw away a pair that I had bought when I was 17. I'm now 34. Yeah, so you do the math! I think I liked keeping them around to tie me to my youth." ~ Megan W.

"I save one particular pair for sexy nights with my husband. He sees them and he knows we're on tonight." ~ Anonymous

"When my ex and I were dating, I sent him a Victoria's Secret panty in the mail every day for a week. He kept them all in their love note envelopes. We broke up and I wear them now. No break-up drama, but when we were dating he would NOT let me wear them as he saw them as little 'treasures'—too cute!!!" ~ Alissa

* * *

From the 1960s, bikini underwear has been worn by women of all ages. In fact, one-third of all women prefer to wear bikinis over any other style of panty.

Why is that? They are comfortable. They are sexy. They cover just enough to allow for the mind to wander without showing all the goods. They move freely with a woman's body and are still very trendy. Women just seem to feel comfortable in them while still feeling womanly and sexy, making them perfect for any occasion and mood.

Trevor never understood the value placed on a pair of panties—and, in this case bikini underwear—until he saw the excitement in the expression on Whitney's face when she held up that lavender pair. It was like she had found her long lost friend. The memories came flooding in and she was smiling from ear to ear. Not only did these panties hold value to Whitney, but for him too.

This was an eye opener for Trevor. No one would have ever thought that through a pair of panties, he would better understand how his wife thinks and what makes her tick. Could this work in other aspects of Whitney's life? In their life? Could he take this information and somehow understand her direction in life and even help her make panty selections based on her mood, her struggles and her goals? Could he learn to better communicate with his life partner through simply understanding the panties she chose from day to day?

This sounded crazy, almost too good to be true and a bit absurd, but this could be powerful if he took the right approach and the time to be observant. Perhaps, if he began to show more compassion and understanding, Whitney would soften her approach in their everyday communication, would be more forthcoming in sharing her thoughts, views and goals—and who knows, she may even be a more eager participant in the bedroom, wanting to reciprocate in all aspects. This may indeed work.

Action Items

Ladies

1. **Let it go!** If you are wearing those priceless bikini panties, you know how you feel. You know that you're relaxed, carefree and enjoying life. Take that feeling and share it with your husband. Don't give him the angst and frustration over the fact that he forgot to empty the garbage this morning and it's trash day. Be smooth, subtle and fun. If he forgot to empty the trash, he already knows; furthermore, he already senses that you're probably going to say something about it. Don't give into the temptation of irritation. Instead, give into the temptation of the panties that are offering that carefree mood. You are wearing them for a reason. Use it.

2. **Instead of seeing the negative, see the positive.** As cliché as this may sound, it is one of the most truthful statements, one that can have the most advantageous affect on any relationship. During your own Bikini Day, show him your fun side. Show him how much you appreciate the small things that he does, and when he does something that you don't particularly care for, let it go (see Action Item #1). A little grace will go a long way. Remember, you are the one with the power. You're the one with those killer panties.

3. **Be a little flirty and have some fun.** Everyone knows that panties can have a universal appeal of being sexy, tantalizing and seductive, no matter what type you're wearing, your size or your age. Panties are panties. Trust me, he is watching you. He knows what you're wearing, so give him the upper hand of knowing that when Bikini Day comes his way, the flirty side is close at hand. The effort may be small, but the reward can be enormous.

Gentlemen

1. **Take notice and offer a compliment or two.** This is a big complaint in women. "He didn't even know I had my hair done or comment on my new dress." Now is your moment to shine in her eyes when you notice her cute bikinis. Now remember, you must not mention them only in a sexual manner (that can come later), but simply speak to her in relation to her beauty and how much you enjoy her. Maybe mention something fun you did the other day as you peer over those adorable panties. Think deep, not just on the surface.

2. **Go with it!** Your lady is wearing that special pair of bikinis and we have already determined that anything can happen. She wants to have fun, maybe go visit some friends, or maybe the two of you can catch an early movie. She may even want to stay in and listen

to some music or work on one of the home projects you have been talking about. Whatever the case may be, just go with it. Take it all in stride and enjoy the moment. Don't fight her on it. If you show the concern and the consideration that all women crave, you will win in the end, further strengthening the bond and the relationship you share.

3. **Create a bikini ritual.** Imagine having something that the two of you do together each time the bikinis come out of the panty drawer. Maybe it means that once she puts them on, you kiss five times in a row. Or it means that she makes the coffee in the morning, or visa versa. What about creating a tradition in which you give her a five minute back rub before she gets dressed and is ready to run off to work? She will love, love, *love* you for that one! Whatever it may be, it's your ritual, the one that you create together. This can be fun—just like the meaning of the panties—and it can be something that will bond the two of you closer together.

Booty Shorts, Anyone?

My wife has an amazing butt, Trevor thought to himself. I remember that week last year in Spain. It was incredible. I wonder if she remembers it the same way I do ... Probably not. Women never see things the same way men do. But I remember. Oh man, do I remember.

Trevor remembered one particular night when the music was playing on the streets and everyone was dancing. The air was warm. The stars were bright and everyone was filled with excitement, having a great time. All this was the backdrop to Trevor and Whitney's own special moment. To their memories being made. For Trevor, it was all about Whitney and how incredibly beautiful, sexy and charming she was. *I was, and still am, a truly lucky man,* he thought.

The way she moved, the way her body touched his, the way she looked with her white wrap-around skirt and red blouse that tied around her waist. She was amazing. Her body was more than he could handle and the way her butt felt under her skirt with those blue booty shorts that made him ...

"Trevor? Trevor?" Whitney called. "Can you help me with this necklace when you finish getting ready, please? I need to get to work a little early today. I have that presentation to give for the advertising director at Nitrelle Cosmetics."

"OK. Give me a sec," replied Trevor. "I'll be right there."

Trevor was still lost in memories of Spain and booty shorts, thinking nothing about a necklace. Nonetheless, he pulled his thoughts together, continued shaving and finished getting himself ready for the day ahead. He too had meetings to attend and knew it would be a hectic day.

When he entered the bedroom, there she was. Whitney, a true thing of beauty, standing in the mirror with a black-and-white, short-sleeved shirt fitting snugly against her body—and, of course, an adorable pair of blue booty shorts. He couldn't believe his eyes. Could this be true? It was like she had read his mind. Instantly, the memories of Spain resurfaced and he was dancing under the stars with his gorgeous wife all over again.

"Come on, silly. Stop drooling," she giggled. "I need you to help me so I can get to work."

"Well, if you weren't so sexy, I'd have nothing to drool over," he responded.

Whitney laughed, shaking her head at her husband's comment, but always flattered and very grateful for the love the two of them shared and the adoration that Trevor had for her.

Without hesitation, he helped her with her necklace while simultaneously running his hand across her butt cheeks, enjoying the view of those booty shorts.

In a faint whisper, Whitney said, "You know you can see more of that later, but right now duty calls," followed by a quick wink.

"Promise?" Trevor asked.

"But of course," she responded and gave him a quick kiss as she left the room and went on her way to work.

Whitney was always very focused when it came to work and her career, and this morning was no different. She was great at what she did and would have both men and women eating out of the palm of her hand whenever she had a presentation to give. There was nothing that stopped her. Her energy was contagious and her passion was undeniable. She had cultivated quite a roster of clientele and executives who would only work with her, no matter how promising other employees were said to be. Truthfully, the secret was her attitude, her love for her job and her drive. She never met a challenge she didn't think she could conquer. She dressed well and always made a lasting impression. Of course, this was a must since she was in the fashion industry.

These traits were part of the reason Trevor loved her so much. "That's my Whitney," he would say when conversing with others during a business gathering. He had seen these characteristics in her from the time they had started dating and now into their marriage. She was a strong woman and he was proud of her.

However, he also saw the other side. The side that was quiet. The one that enjoyed not being a part of the crowd and loved to read a book and listen to music. The one that liked alone time and could even get quite frustrated when she felt unsure about something, perhaps a situation at work. He alone was privy to those traits.

Trevor always admired Whitney for her diligence and fortitude. He often wondered where those qualities came from. He too was quite successful in his job, but Whitney just seemed to handle everything with ease. There had to be something more to this "having it all together" attitude than meets the eye. So Trevor started on his quest for answers. He began with things that he had observed over the past couple of months, thinking about times when she was sad, or when she was happy and feeling strong and confident. He wanted to better understand his wife, and in this process, he knew he'd begin understanding himself and their relationship in a much deeper way.

As Trevor put some effort into this exercise, he thought about the last time he and Whitney went to visit her parents. She was happy and seemed to enjoy herself. But there was always that side of her that was eager to leave because she always had something else to do. Also, he seemed to notice that each time she had a presentation to give at work, she was focused, determined and driven, just as she had been this morning. And what about the times when she was feeling flirty, relaxed and looking forward to a day out with friends? Whatever the case may have been, one thing that remained constant was Whitney's demeanor in each of these scenarios—confident, passionate, happy. Why was that? What did it mean?

Lastly, he thought back to the other day when they had stayed home from work to clean out the garage and go to the beach. He mulled over the details in his mind until he suddenly realized how Whitney's demeanor had changed once she found those lavender bikinis. She was thrilled, to say the least. And, to take it a step further, she was fun, excited and completely stress free.

Could the panties that Whitney wears each day be the solution? he wondered. *Are there certain types of panties that she wears when she is acting and behaving in a certain way? If so, does she recognize it? Does she even know it's happening?*

He was definitely going to find out.

When Trevor returned home after work, Whitney was standing in the kitchen preparing a salad to go with dinner.

"How was your day, honey?" Whitney asked.

"Great. I got so much accomplished," Trevor replied. "In fact, we were just approved to fill three new positions and I'll be getting an intern in a few weeks to assist with some design work for the advertising department. I'm pretty excited about it. We are all swamped and it should take a load off our plates—provided they know what they're doing." He chuckled to himself.

"That's awesome. I know things have been stressful and I hate to see you feeling overwhelmed. I'm glad it came through for the intern," Whitney replied.

"How did your presentation go with Nitrelle?"

"Amazing! They loved my proposal. The director said he would get with me next week to finalize the plans."

Did I expect anything less? Trevor thought to himself. He knew just how great she was at what she did—not to mention beautiful.

"That's awesome. I'm so proud of you. I knew you could do it," he responded with excitement. "We need to celebrate tonight. How about a glass of wine with dinner and a little music to lighten the mood and then an early night?" He gave a playful look toward the bedroom. "I know you didn't forget what you promised this morning, did you?"

"Of course not! I told you that we would clean out the closets in the guest room this evening, change the sheets on the bed and take Digger for a walk to the park. Isn't that right?"

She started laughing hysterically. Whitney loved to mess with Trevor. It was her way of keeping him on his toes.

Trevor gave her a sarcastic look, shaking his head, and then joined her in laughter.

"Oh! You mean about seeing more of those panties from earlier today. Am I right?" She sashayed past Trevor to lean on the counter.

"Yep. You got it," he said with a smile and a look in his eye that only Whitney could know.

Trevor couldn't help but think about his new mission. He was eager to learn the secrets of Mrs. Whitney Wright. He wanted to know all there was to know and to learn how he could better partner with her as her husband, her lover and her friend. He was her biggest supporter, whether she knew it or not. With the excitement of so many new thoughts swimming around in his head, he was just as excited to lay his eyes on those blue booty shorts once again. The image of her in them this morning had not left his mind all day, nor had his ideas about the meaning behind the panties either.

And now, since she had returned from work, he had data. She wore blue. She wore booty shorts. She was driven. She was focused. She succeeded. Could it have been the power of the panties and how she felt in them? Maybe. Only time would tell. In the meantime, he had some panties to go and see.

* * *

"I love my cheeky panties because they make me feel sexy and secure." ~ Anonymous

"I have one pair of panties that I use when I need to get into my confident mood. When I have a big negotiation at work or have to do a presentation in front of many people, just knowing that I have them on makes me straighten my shoulders and get a bounce in my step." ~ Louise A.

"Booty shorts are a state of mind, not just a piece of clothing!" ~ Anonymous

"When I met my husband his first response was 'You have a nice a—.' What I said ... 'Man, you're crazy.' His answer was 'Crazy for you.' I had on my special booty shorts panties. It got the conversation going. I now call them my lucky panties." ~ Connie Sue

* * *

Booty shorts became popular in the 1990s, mostly with teenage girls and college students. They were associated with youthfulness, a fun and outgoing nature and a sense of adventure and assertive tendencies. As time went on, women of all ages, sizes and nationalities chose to follow suit. In the year 2000, a huge jump in popularity was noticed when Cameron Diaz sported her pair of classic booty shorts in the blockbuster hit, *Charlie's Angels*.

Don't believe me? Enter YouTube!
(https://youtu.be/PXEurnT09iw)

These trendy undies were being welcomed by women for the reasons already mentioned, in addition to their comfort and their ability to hide panty lines underneath certain styles of clothing. And men? They welcomed these fashionable panties due to their sex appeal, flirtatious value and their ability to transform their lady into an adorable and seductive tease while staying true to her feminine beauty.

Trevor and Whitney had a great relationship, but like any couple, they had their share of problems too. What always seemed to keep them going and growing was their determination to meet each challenge head on and stay open to change whenever needed.

This mindset was what led Trevor to begin examining the power of panties and how they affected Whitney from day to day. He wanted to know if her path was and could be directed by her panty selection. If so, he would definitely have more insight and understanding of her moods and how she would go about her day.

Of course, nothing is that perfect 100% of the time and life does not offer a "cookie cutter" solution to its problems. There are too many factors that force us to change our natural direction from day to day and in turn lend to a response much different than originally planned. Nonetheless, he would certainly know more than he did without this knowledge. In the meantime, "Booty Shorts, Anyone?"

Action Items

Ladies

1. **Play the Match Game.** Remember when you'd go out on a date and would want to look especially sexy for some intimate games of fun? When you'd want to ensure that everything was matching during your spontaneous strip show (the one that really wasn't spontaneous because you planned on showing all the goods anyway)? You knew your significant other would just love to see you in your matching bra and panties with some stockings and a pair of high heels that you knew would knock him off his feet. But if you weren't looking for that reaction, you'd just wear that regular purple bra with some yellow-and-red striped panties, white stockings and royal blue pumps, the ones that you had to purchase for your cousin's wedding. Now you tell me: would the reaction be the same? Of course not (well, at least not usually). He would think you'd lost your mind and that night of romance you just knew was going to happen would suddenly be spent watching reruns of *Seinfeld*.

   Well, imagine this. You're sitting in your living room after a long day at work, having just enjoyed a nice dinner and watching (but of course) reruns of *Seinfeld*, when he decides he wants some "dessert." The two of you begin kissing gently, then the hands start moving, the heat is rising, he begins undressing you, excited for the next step, and *voila*. There you are in a matching bra and panty set (and, of course, they are your "to-die-for" booty shorts) that makes his heart stop. All he's thinking about is *How did she know we were going to do something? I had no idea she had this on!* You made his night, trust me, and he will be forever grateful. So my advice to you? Mix it up a bit by not mixing it up. Play the match game and have some real fun.

2. **Don't be scared!** We have all wanted to try something new and different, but for various reasons we get scared. We come up with every excuse under the sun, from "I'm too fat" to "I'm too skinny" or "I'm too tall" or "I'm too short." Well, ladies, let me say this: no matter what you may think your flaws are, your thoughts are much more exaggerated than the truth. Most men absolutely love it when you live on the edge a bit and do something you don't normally do. So if it's booty shorts that intrigue you, then booty shorts it is. Buy a couple of pairs and wear those bad boys. You might be pleasantly surprised.

3. **Create a new you.** We've always been told, whether by our parents or others along the line, that we can do anything we set our mind to. I believe this to be true. Some things are just a little more difficult than others. In the case of panties, we know that certain types of panties can make us feel differently. It's that limbic

system buried deep in the cerebrum that tells us how to feel and speaks to our emotions. And, of course, we can teach that limbic system how to react more favorably, giving us results that we want. Since booty shorts have a reputation of being worn by ladies who are fun, sexy and spontaneous, why not be that (unless you already are, of course) at home and at work? Your booty shorts can take you to a new level—and you might even enjoy the ride!

Gentlemen

1. **Show some encouragement.** Whether your lady is a booty shorts girl or not, sometimes a little encouragement goes a long way. Maybe you've seen the same few pairs for quite some time now and you'd like to see a change. Or maybe your girl doesn't wear booty shorts, but you'd love to see her in a pair. In either of these cases, take a trip down to the mall, visit the undies aisle and see what sparks your interest. Let her know just how beautiful and sexy she is. You might even get a fashion show.

2. **Have a skivvies game night.** As I'm sure it's already been proven, you love seeing your lady in her panties and probably would love it even more if you could see them more often. So make it happen! Have an evening where you play your favorite game in your skivvies, both of you. It doesn't matter what it is. It could be

Monopoly for all intents and purposes (but Strip Poker probably wouldn't work, since you're already down to the bare minimum). The objective is to create some fun and do something totally different, getting away from the mundane and routine evenings. Also, remember this: booty shorts, by and large, equate to a woman who is fun, sexy and spontaneous. So you have nothing to lose. Let the games begin.

3. **Impress her with your ability to read her mood and body language.** Now this might be a bit tough, but if you're intuitive, you'll get it. The rule is that you can't watch her get dressed because you can't know what type of panties she puts on for the day. What you are going to do is "read" her mood and demeanor, whether it's in the morning before you two leave for the day, or in the evening when she gets home. As you begin, keep in mind that the majority of women who wear booty shorts are charismatic, social, friendly and go-getters.

When you first start talking with her, you will want to have some casual conversation for a bit and see how she's feeling. Is she bubbly, more so than usual? Is she relaxed yet still ready to conquer the world? Or, if she's just returned home from work, is she excited and talkative about her day and eager for the two of you to have a fun evening, strutting around with her sexy, cute self? If you answered *Yes* to any of these questions, chances are she may be wearing a pair of adorable booty shorts. You can then reveal *how* you know this. If you're right—and chances will be that you are—she will be shocked to know that you took such notice, that you've been paying attention to her and taking the time to understand what makes her tick. If you passed the test, it's just the beginning to showing her what you can really do.

Thong Song

Over the past week, Trevor spent time researching his theory about the connection between his wife's behavior and the panties she wore. He read over various Internet articles about the subject, but wasn't able to find any books on the subject. He knew that he would need to do most of the research himself and even possibly recruit some of his friends. Nonetheless, he felt like it was making sense. Not only could he predict his wife's moods through her panty selection, but he could even play a part in the success of her day based on his gentle suggestions. Furthermore, Trevor began to wonder how far this theory would go—could it be possible to even change Whitney's path and career progression?

Trevor was indeed learning quite a bit about the subject. After careful consideration, he decided to talk to a couple of friends about it one night while meeting up to watch *Monday Night Football*. He wasn't sure what they would think or if they would just see him as some weirdo talking about panties, putting too much time into something that probably didn't mean anything at all or have any validity to it whatsoever.

Nonetheless, he was going to give it a whirl.

It was 7:00 when the guys started arriving for the game. Trevor had bought some pizza and chips and the guys were bringing the drinks. Everyone had been talking about the game at work earlier that day as predictions were being made for the playoffs, and tonight was destined to be a tough game. It would be the Philadelphia Eagles against the Denver Broncos, and of course, Trevor was for the Eagles, along with a couple of the other guys.

"I'm really looking forward to this game tonight," said Trevor. "I just want to rub it in Adam's face when the Eagles stomp all over the Broncos."

"Hey, Trevor," said Brenton. "Speaking of Adam. Did you hear him talking earlier today about the merger that's going to be happening with Inlite and Sungrey?"

"I don't believe anything Adam says," Harrison chimed in. "I think it's just rumors. It gives him something to say when he should really be doing his job."

"I don't know," said Trevor. "Sometimes—and I do mean *sometimes*—Adam actually has some good insight. He's just an oddball, for sure. I wouldn't worry about it unless we start to hear more from the higher ups."

"I guess you're right," said Brenton. "I just don't want to be blindsided like they have a way of doing from time to time."

"Yeah, I don't dare say anything to my wife about it. She'll freak out and then she'll have us up and moving before we even know if it's for certain," Justin said half sarcastically while overlaid with a bit of truth.

Everyone broke out in laughter. They all knew exactly how Justin's wife could be at the mere thought of uncertainty or change. She was definitely the panicky type, while Justin was completely the opposite.

"I wish Bree could be more laid back and not get so uptight about things. Everything has to be planned out a year in advance in order for her to be OK. I swear, pretty soon she'll be planning how many times I can go to the bathroom each day," Justin said in a very tired and frustrated voice.

Again, everyone broke out in hysterics. Bree was a tough cookie. Very loving, but still tough.

"The other day, she was telling me that my sister was planning on coming to visit in the summer and couldn't understand why she didn't have the dates already solidified. I told her not to worry about it because it was still several months away. And do you know what she said? She said, 'Well, I will need to know what we will be eating because I know your sister is picky.' I just looked at her and couldn't believe she was serious. I explained there was plenty of time to plan, but what can I say? She always has her panties in a bunch about something."

When Trevor heard Justin make that statement, he knew that was his ticket in. The stage had been set for him to let them in on his new "panty theory" and to get their opinions.

"With that statement in mind," Trevor began, "have any of you ever thought about the whole 'panties-in-a-bunch' thing before? I mean, have you ever wondered if there really is something to why women wear the panties they wear and if it could maybe even shape their moods and behavior?"

"The only thing I know about 'shaping' anything is how sexy my wife looks in that thong she wears," said Harrison. "I just love it."

"What I mean, Harrison, is what do you think the psychology is behind it?" Trevor asked.

"Where is this coming from, man?" asked Brenton. "The only thing I really equate certain panties to is a great night of sex."

Trevor was getting frustrated and had even started to resent the fact that he had brought it up. He was getting nowhere, and fast.

"Wait a minute," added Justin. "Let's think about this. If there could possibly be any way that I could better understand Bree and 'shape' her moods and behavior, as you put it, then I'm in. I want to hear more."

Now the ball was rolling. Trevor was beginning to feel that there was hope and he could take advantage of this moment and get some valuable insight.

"Harrison," Trevor started.

"Yes?"

"You stated that you love how Lisa looks in her thong."

"This is getting weird," Brenton interrupted. "What Sophia wears is for me and that's it. I'm not comfortable talking about the types of panties our wives wear, especially with the three of you," he chuckled.

"Bear with me," Trevor replied. "I know it's weird, but I really think there's something to it. Try not to think of it in an all-sexual manner."

"OK," Brenton replied, "but you need to get to the point."

Once again, Trevor had the floor.

"Back to you Harrison," Trevor started. "And back to the thong. Does Lisa wear different types of panties?"

"Yeah," Harrison replied, still a bit puzzled.

"Does she act differently when she wears a thong versus other types of panties?" Trevor asked.

"I haven't really noticed," Harrison responded. "I haven't really paid it much attention."

"OK, well, just try to think about it the best you can for now," Trevor suggested. "How does she act when you know that she is wearing a thong? What are her actions?"

"I guess I would have to say that she is confident," Harrison started, "but then again, that's how she is normally, so I don't know if that counts. She speaks her mind more freely. She's straightforward. Seems to be sure of herself and demonstrates just how incredibly intelligent she is, holding nothing back. And, now that I think about it, she always seems to wear a thong when she wears her business pantsuits and is preparing for a big meeting. Hmmm. Interesting." Harrison sat there, deeply thinking about all that he had said.

"Got it," Trevor said, interrupting Harrison's thoughts.

"So if this is true," Justin chimed in, "Bree should never wear another thong again. She's already way too confident—and controlling, too."

Everyone burst out laughing, but understood completely where he was coming from.

"Actually," Trevor said, "she should probably be wearing bikinis ninety-nine percent of the time, but more of that to follow later."

Trevor had certainly peaked everyone's interest with his theories and his research. Furthermore, they each wanted to understand more in hopes of better communicating with their wives, as odd as it all seemed. They were beginning to ask questions and compare notes with one another about the types of panties their wives wore and how their attitudes changed. They wanted to know about G-strings, bikinis and even if any of their wives went "commando." There was so much to learn, but one thing that Trevor did know was that he had stumbled upon something—and it was something big.

* * *

"Put a thong on once and didn't notice I had the leg around the waist." ~ Tina

"Wearing a thong makes me feel more attractive and self-assured." ~ Anonymous

"My husband remembers I was wearing yellow smiley-face panties the first time we were intimate." ~ Anonymous

* * *

According to my study, 28% of women wear thongs for various occasions, and there are many schools of thought surrounding women wearing them. Some will say that a woman who wears a thong is easy, flirtatious, extremely sexually outgoing and even intimidating. This may or may not be true for you specifically, but to a point, don't we all want to be these things from time to time, when it's most appropriate?

When the thong began its rise and landed into the drawers of ladies near and far, around the mid- to late-90s and the early 2000s, some women had a hard time adjusting to this style and couldn't figure out why other women were wearing them. These small pieces of fabric could not constitute a pair of women's undergarments, but women were loving them. The world of underwear had now delivered something that was not only sexy and could speak to the woman's strong, courageous and sensual self, but they were also practical, came in every color imaginable, were comfortable and kept those tight skirts and pants free from panty lines.

As this style's popularity spread, women of all ages began wearing them. These skimpy, stylish panties were not only for the younger generations—even women in their 70s were finding some excitement in the latest trend. Think about this for a moment. If someone in their 70s can wear a thong, then anyone can and should never feel ashamed or uncomfortable. My hat goes off to those women who are free to be themselves no matter what their age may be.

So ladies, what about you? How does wearing a thong make you feel? Have you given it much thought? Do you wear a thong for certain occasions? Maybe a night out with the hubby? Or maybe a big event at work or the kid's soccer game? To take it a step further, do you think that if you were to wear your favorite thong in specific settings, it could change your direction for the day or even your entire path, making it more advantageous, productive and exciting?

It is indeed something to think about.

In the story, Trevor is on a mission to prove this theory to be true. In the cases of the bikini, the booty shorts and even the thong, his theory is indeed proving to be true, even in the eyes of his buddies. Assuredly, he will learn more as he continues his research and continues his interaction with Whitney.

Action Items

Ladies

For this chapter, you will need to think more deeply about your panty selections and be more deliberate about your actions.

Complete each of the questions below and see if you find that your thoughts and feelings about wearing a thong are any different than what you may have thought in the past.

1. If you wear a thong, what is your reason for wearing it?

2. How often do you wear a thong?

3. How does wearing a thong make you feel? Answer honestly. Think of as many feelings and emotions as possible and write them down.

4. As you pick out your panties for the day, give it some thought. Think about your plans. What are you doing? Who will you be seeing? Is it a day at the office or a day of leisure? If you had originally intended on wearing something other than a thong, change it up. Put on that cute thong instead and see how you feel. Think about it during the day and take a self-inventory on how the day is going. Is it fun or dreary?

Are you tired or excited? Did you accomplish things you didn't think you would? Did you feel confident, ready to take on the world, or were you more laid back and going with the status quo?

Depending on how you answered those questions, you may find that wearing a thong is exactly what you needed for the day—and then again, maybe it isn't. In either case, if you were honest and truly put thought into the exercise, you will have learned more about yourself and a simple pair of panties than you thought possible. You will have learned what works for you and what you are seeking to accomplish for each day.

And who knows? Maybe wearing a thong isn't even for you. Only time will tell, and only you have the answer to that question.

Gentlemen

You've now covered three different types of panties and are probably a bit more versed in the subject than when you started. Hopefully you've discovered some things about your wife or girlfriend that have given you further insight into who she is in relation to her panties.

For the questions below, you will want to take notes to review later and to also share with her when the time comes.

1. When your wife or girlfriend puts on a thong in the morning, what is her mood like? What are her plans for the day? Does she say anything about how they look, or walk around the room waiting for you to give her a smile and nod of approval? Is she looking to be sexy, strong or confident? Maybe it's all of the above. Use as many words as needed to describe everything about her in her thong, from moods to looks.

2. Think about your wife or girlfriend's plans for the day. What are her goals and what is she looking to accomplish? Now is your time to swoop in and make your grand panty suggestion. Don't tell her why. Keep that to yourself, at least for now. Just let her know how beautiful and sexy she is. Then, at the end of the day, take note about her mood and what she did and accomplished. This will give you some traction for further suggestions later and it will also give you some talking points when you share your new knowledge about her—the woman of your dreams.

3. Thong Song—this is your chance to be creative. And don't say you're not! Everyone has a little bit of creativity in them. You're going to create a song, something fun, about her wearing a thong. It does not need to be long, so don't worry. You're going to use words in this song about her moods, her emotions, how she looks, the colors of her thongs and why she wears them. This will be your own cue for her when

you know she's about to do something that will warrant her wearing a thong. It will be your fun song to sing through the house when you are looking for a specific result from the panties. Have fun with this. Make it short, simple and sweet. You'll be surprised at the reaction you'll get.

Granny Panties— Don't Be Fooled

The weather was seeming to change a bit, with clouds in the sky and a gentle, cool breeze blowing through the chimes hanging from the back porch. Whitney loved this weather. She always welcomed the fresh air flowing through the house. It created the perfect atmosphere for some light weekend housework, and today was no different.

Whitney was up early, taking full advantage of the day ahead. She had lots to get done and would also be meeting up with some of her friends at the dog park later. The dog park was always part of the weekend routine and Digger never let her forget it. Trevor was still in bed catching up on some much needed sleep from the past week.

Although she was looking forward to the day, she hadn't slept too well. She couldn't figure out what was going on with Trevor. He had been acting quite strange and unusually attentive, wanting to be more involved in her day and in understanding how she was doing. Of course she was flattered—for the most part. Who wouldn't be, when their husband was waking up early to help with the morning rush or even excited when he knew they had a big day ahead? It was almost as though he could read her mind. It was just weird—plain weird—and she wanted to know what was going on.

It was around 1:00 when Whitney arrived at the dog park. Sophia and Lisa were already there and Bree had texted that she was running a little late, but was on her way. Bree and Justin didn't have a dog, but she liked coming to the park to hang out and chat for a bit.

"Hi, ladies," Whitney said as she approached Sophia and Lisa. They sat on the bench watching their dogs playing with their other canine friends.

"Hi," they both responded in unison.

"There's a bunch out here today," Sophia added. "I think it's the weather. No one wanted to be out here when it was so hot, but now that the temperature has cooled down, everyone decided to get out of the house."

"I completely agree!" Whitney released Digger to go and play with his friends.

"Did you get your normal weekend housework done this morning?" Sophia asked half-jokingly. Everyone knew that Whitney was very predictable about many things, and weekend housework was definitely one of them.

"But of course," Whitney responded. "I always have to get my stuff done. But I'm just kind of tired this morning. I didn't sleep well last night."

"Oh … I guess Trevor had you up all night?" Sophia said sarcastically, laughing herself silly.

"No, Sophia," Whitney retorted, laughing too. "I was just doing a lot of thinking, mostly about Trevor."

"Hi, Bree," Lisa said as Bree approached the bench. "How are you?"

"I'm good," said Bree. "Glad to be out of the house! Justin was driving me crazy. I told him to stop opening different cereal boxes before the other ones are empty."

Everyone started laughing. Everyone knew that Bree could be tough on Justin and always had to have things a certain way. But the one good thing about her was that no matter what time of day or night, she was always available to help her friends and family. She was amazing in many ways.

"I'm sure it's not *that* big of a deal," Lisa stated. "It's not the end of the world, Bree."

"To me it is! If you open too many boxes, one box is bound to get stale," Bree explained. Then, stopping to think about it for a moment, she even had to laugh at herself.

"OK. Enough of your cereal box drama, Miss Bree," Sophia said. "Whitney was talking to us about Trevor and saying that he's been acting weird."

"Oh, sorry," Bree said. "I understand—Justin's been acting different, too."

"Really?" Whitney asked.

"Totally," Bree replied.

"OK, Whitney. Back to your story. Is everything OK?" Lisa asked in a concerned voice. "You guys aren't having any problems or anything, right?"

"No. Nothing like that," Whitney responded. "In fact, Trevor has been more attentive than ever. We've been married for a while now, and we are in a very comfortable place and supportive of one another. Of course we have our share of ups and down like anyone else, but nothing alarming."

Everyone was trying to figure out where this was going, but as the conversation continued, they would soon find out that they each were experiencing some of the same things with their own husbands.

"Then what is it?" Sophia asked, her concern growing.

Whitney continued explaining. "It all started a few weeks back when we played hooky from work. We decided to clean out some boxes in the garage and do some rearranging when we came across one of my boxes filled with old clothes. To my surprise—and a little embarrassment—I had old panties in there from college."

They all started laughing and making funny comments and jokes.

"Did Trevor get weird, like they were purchased for some other guy or something?" Bree asked.

"Oh, no. Nothing like that," Whitney laughed. "He was just interested. I was so excited to see them. I think that's what perked his interest. I practically passed out when I found this pair of bikinis that I absolutely adored. They were lavender with a tiny bow right on the front. I tried to play it off, but when we finished cleaning, he asked me to wear them the rest of the day."

"Really?" Sophia asked. "Yeah. I would've thought that was weird, too."

"Yep," Whitney replied. "It was no big deal to me. I was just glad it didn't matter to him one way or another."

Whitney sat pondering her next statement before she shared her thoughts.

"Ever since that day, or shortly thereafter, it's like Trevor's been watching me, asking me weird questions about how I'm feeling, if I need anything and wondering about my day at work. Don't get me wrong. He's always been thoughtful in that way, but this is on a whole new level. And since this so-called change, it's almost like he's inside my mind. Like he knows what I'm thinking and then has some weird way of 'helping' me get through it. I don't know what to say about it. It's just got me baffled."

"That's crazy," Lisa stated. "I do know that since the guys got together last week for *Monday Night Football*, Harrison has been asking strange questions, too. It all started with me wearing a thong. He began making statements about how I act when I have a thong on and telling me that he knows if I'm wearing one by the way I'm acting. I just looked at him like he was nuts, but inside I knew he was right. But how can that be? How could he know? So I decided to start wearing other types of panties to see what would happen."

"Me too," Whitney added. "I even started wearing some granny panties the other day. I figured he would get uninterested in this whole 'panty thing' of his. But it didn't work."

"I wasn't going to say anything," Sophia chimed in, "but Brenton has always been about the sex when it comes to panties. He has *his* favorite ones that I wear, but beyond that, he has never given my panty selection the time of day ... until lately."

"What's changed?" Whitney asked.

"The same stuff that you guys have been talking about," Sophia replied.

"The same is true for me, too," Bree added. "In fact, Justin keeps making statements about how much he loves seeing me in bikinis, which is really weird because he always loved it when I wore a thong in the past. I don't know where that came from."

"So back to this 'granny panty' thing," Whitney stated.

Everyone sat in anticipation of what Whitney was going to share.

"When I put on a pair of my granny panties, which I must admit I totally love, I was expecting Trevor to ask me why I was wearing them. But, of course, I was wrong. He said, 'Ooh, those are nice, babe! I love the way they shape your butt.' I couldn't believe it. I was looking to curb his interest—not *peak* his interest. He went on to tell me how sexy I am and that he loves how they accentuate my beautiful curves. I thought I was gonnna gag. Is he for real? Really? What is he thinking? I thought these granny panties were my 'safe' panties. You know, the ones that get you no attention from your man."

"Oh, my goodness," Sophia cut in. "I wore some granny panties just today! When Brenton saw me getting dressed, he came over and gave me a kiss and told me I looked unbelievably sexy and wanted me to make sure I wore them later for bed. He went so far as to tell me that

Calvin Klein models wear them. What? How does he even know that? This whole thing is weird."

"I agree," Bree nodded. "Maybe our husbands should stop hanging out. Then again, maybe they should hang out more."

Everyone started laughing, each pondering the truth behind Bree's statement.

"One thing I do know," Lisa added, "is that I love my granny panties. There's something about the comfort in them and the way they can hide all the 'stuff,' if you know what I mean. They're functional, and I love how my body feels in them."

"I do know what you mean," Whitney said.

"I guess we need to keep watching this new panty revelation our husbands seem to have discovered," Bree said.

"For sure," Whitney agreed. "In the meantime, I'm going to keep wearing my granny panties—at least for a few more days—and see where it all goes."

* * *

*"My favorite type of panties are usually
granny panties due to them being comfortable
and feeling as if you have none on."*
~ Anonymous

*"My 15-year-old (but still a Casanova)
mongrel doggie went over to visit the
purebred, in-heat bitch next door and would
not come when I called. I ran after him in my
'granny panties' (couldn't there be a better
name for sensible undies?!?) and my nightie
and grabbed him, but he didn't have his collar
on and just kept dropping to the ground. So I
took off my panties, put them around his
neck and used them as a collar and leash to
drag him home. They were old, pink and full
of holes so that was their last use. He did not
feel guilty at all, the old Lothario!"* ~ Maggie*

*"A day home in front of the fire requires
granny panties with the most holes."* ~
Anonymous

* * *

Whitney and her friends were just beginning to find that there may be more to a pair of panties than they had ever imagined. Each of the ladies had found that their husbands were beginning to take special interest in their panty selections—even granny panties. They had always thought, or perhaps had even heard, that granny panties were seemingly nonessential to men and would probably go as far as to say that they'd hope their wife or girlfriend would never wear them.

However, they were quickly learning that not only did their husbands like granny panties, but they seemed to understand that granny panties, along with other styles, seemed to carry their own sense of value that was dependent upon their wife's mood and plans for the day. These panties had a specific role that they were designed to fulfill, and if men could understand their significance, they could equally understand the "why" behind the panties.

When we hear people talk of "big knickers," "full bloomers," or in this case "granny panties," we often imagine a pair of undies that look extremely ugly, are tattered, saggy and out of shape, and are being worn by an older woman—and I do mean *old*—who is also out of shape and scared to even look at herself in the mirror.

Furthermore, we think of the scene from the 2001 blockbuster hit, *Bridget Jones's Diary*, in which Renée Zellweger quickly ditches her black granny panties prior to her big date. Her goal is to look sexy and clearly she would not be caught dead wearing something her grandmother would have worn some fifty years prior.

Unfortunately, these images have been imprinted in our minds and have become the classic stereotype of granny panties portrayed by the media—but don't be fooled!

Granny panties are making their way back up the panty chain, with more women choosing this so-called "out-of-date" style over the more provocative, lacy and skimpy choices available. Not only is this being seen with the modern-day woman, but Hollywood is certainly playing a role in the surge of granny panty sales due to the variety of top entertainers showing off their knickers under gorgeous gowns on high-fashion runways and at red carpet events. Apparently, these panties are not only for a woman's most relaxed moments, but also for her most done up moments too.

Granny panties have undoubtedly been the go-to choice over the years for a woman wanting to chill, as we know, but there are other reasons, too, that these knickers have held their place in the panty drawer of women near and far.

- They can fit any sized woman.
- They are cute and appealing.
- They fit comfortably, hold in all that they need to and add firmness to the curves.
- To top it off, women are choosing granny panties over other types of skivvies at an increased rate of 11% according to my study.

Although these knickers may have started generations ago, it will be generations to follow that will continue to embrace this style in the most practical manner and for any occasion.

And let's not forget about the men. They too are finding granny panties to be sexy, attractive and stylish. Some men have stated that a woman who wears granny panties is more down to earth, secure and conscientious of the relationship she's in, not focused on outward appearances to gain her sense of value and self esteem.

Also, with "the goods" being covered under engaging fabrics and colors, with no further exposure or vulnerability, the thought of *What's in the Panties?* becomes one that is even more tantalizing and exciting.

Action Items

Ladies

1. **Dress up the grannies!** Instead of putting on your normal sexy panties for a night of romance, have some fun and dress up the granny panties with something he wouldn't even imagine. Maybe wear a short skirt that shows the bottoms of you grannies, or a cute bra that matches those gems with a button-down shirt that is only buttoned at the bottom, followed by some knee socks, tennies and pigtails. Just do something sexy and fun that he would never think possible with a pair of uncanny grannies. Show him just how sexy you can be in whatever you wear.

2. **Play the color game.** Ask your husband or boyfriend what his seven favorite colors are (one for each day of the week). Then, go to your favorite store and pick up seven adorable pairs of granny panties that you'll wear for the week. As you wear a pair each day, write a little note telling your man why he's so special to you and share a memory with him about how wonderful he makes you feel.

3. **Dare to be different.** Create a character (and give it a name) that signifies the person you dare to be. If you strive to be more confident, let that be your character (i.e. Confident Carol, or something not even related to

your name). If it's outgoing, that will be your character. You get the picture. The idea of this exercise is to visualize that character and how they will go through each day. How will they talk? How will they interact with people? How will they be as a wife or girlfriend? A mother? Then, put that character into action, even in the areas of role playing in the bedroom. You will soon start to notice that the panties you're wearing will signify that character and you will begin to strengthen areas in your personality that you never deemed possible.

Gentlemen

1. **Start your night of romance out with her wearing granny panties.** Don't wait until you know she's got the best of the best on underneath that dress or those jeans. You want to show her how much you appreciate her in whatever she wears, and sometimes some granny panties will do just the trick.

2. **Synchronize the day with matching undies.** Granny panties are the equivalent of a man's white briefs. Surprise her by grabbing a pair of her skivvies and laying them out for her to wear with her outfit for the day and make sure you're wearing your tighty-whities when she enters the room. You want her to see the fun in you.

3. **Use power words.** Choose five power words that define the personality of your wife or girlfriend. Use these words randomly when you know she's wearing her granny panties. This is where the power of suggestion will come in to play. As you begin using these words to describe her (i.e. strong, courageous, charming, etc.) she will begin to possess those traits. As the old saying goes, "Choose your words wisely."

Legally Commando

Digger was at the back door whining to come back in. He'd been outside chewing on a bone and, of course, seeing what he could dig up. Whitney and Trevor had created an area in the backyard that was designated for Digger and his bone excavations. From time to time, they would bury a bone or two and let Digger find them. It seemed to help keep him out of the flower garden.

"Are you ready to come back in, boy?" Trevor asked as he opened the door for the very excited dog.

With a wag of the tail, Digger was back inside and lying on his cushion next to the sofa.

"He's so spoiled," Whitney said, shaking her head and smiling.

"I know," Trevor replied, "but it's your fault. He has you wrapped around his finger—or should I say, paw."

"That's not true," she retorted.

Trevor just gave her a look as if to say, "Really?" but chose not to say anything. He figured the look said enough.

"Well, he is just so sweet and—"

"Spoiled," Trevor finished, and they both started laughing.

"With this weather changing as of late, I'm glad that it's a bit warm today," Whitney said.

"Yeah, me too," Trevor agreed. "It's going to make for a nice day at the picnic."

"Without a doubt," Whitney said.

Tribe Designs' annual picnic was a big event that was held in the first part of October each year. It was definitely not the average run-of-the-mill picnic like that of many other companies. This was as five-star as you could get with an outdoor family-fun event. From the lowest position to highest, everyone came ready to eat lots of food catered by the best BBQ restaurant around, participate in games and win cash prizes and listen to live music. Furthermore, a brief talk about the company's direction for the upcoming year would be discussed, and at the end of the day everyone would sit around on palette cushions eating toasted marshmallows and share one thing that they were most grateful for over the past year. It was always a special time, and even the young children participated in this sharing experience.

Tribe Designs was a family-owned and driven company and it showed every year at the annual picnic. No other company strived to help employees achieve a solid work-life/family-life balance like that of this company, and they had been brilliant in their approach and success in doing so. Whitney always felt blessed to be a part of such a great company and was excited to see where it would take her in her career path.

"I think I'm going to wear that white sundress with the red flowers on it," she said. "It's so comfortable and the day is perfect for it."

"That'll be nice, honey," Trevor replied. "You know I love to see you in dresses."

Whitney turned toward him and smiled.

"I'm going to wear those shorts you gave me for my birthday," he said.

"Sounds great!"

Trevor couldn't help but wonder what Whitney would be wearing under that dress, but chose not to ask. It seemed that Whitney had become a little annoyed with his sudden interest in her panties. She was only used to him talking about undies when they were going to have sex, and now suddenly it seemed that he had more to say about the subject. Apparently, she thought it was strange. In theory, one would think she'd be happy that panties are not only about sex, but on the flip side a woman enjoys having that one something (in this case, the panties) that's secret, only known to her. Trevor was infringing upon her "panty space," or at least that's what she thought.

As Whitney was getting ready for the picnic, she was thinking about some of the things her friends had been talking about at the dog park. It was strange that all of them had been experiencing some of the same feelings of confusion related to the subject of panties and their husbands' sudden interest in them. It didn't seem to make much sense. But one thing that Whitney did notice was that she was beginning to become more curious about her panties as well, wondering if they were somehow impacting her day-to-day decisions. It was something she had never thought about much, but thanks to Trevor, she was definitely taking inventory.

As Whitney pulled her pantry drawer out, ready to grab a pair of white bikinis, she stopped for a moment. She thought long and hard about which pair to wear and how she would feel when she put them on. Of course, the white would match her dress, but what else was there to it? She wanted to base her decision on what she'd be doing for the day and how she'd be feeling, or want to feel.

Then it hit her.

Why not go commando today? It's not like it's illegal, she thought to herself, laughing nervously about the idea.

This was definitely something new for Whitney. She had never really gone with nothing before, outside of going to bed at night. She had read articles about it, though, and a lot of women chose to do it when they wore skirts because it eliminated rubbing and feeling uncomfortable—plus it was apparently very hygienic.

She continued to contemplate this new idea. To take it a step further, Trevor wouldn't have anything to say about the panties she was wearing. In fact, she was going to make sure he didn't even see her get dressed. He'd have no idea what was underneath.

When Whitney had finished getting ready, she took inventory as to how she felt. It was a weird feeling not having any panties on, knowing she would be going out in public. She almost felt like some creepy person you tell your kids to stay away from. On the flip side, this new "commando" thing was intriguing. It almost provided a sense of freedom. She felt like she had nothing to hide. What you see is what you get, but not literally.

She stood in front of her long mirror in the bedroom, turning from side to side and then looking at the back of her dress with her head over her shoulder. She wanted to see if anyone would be able to tell she didn't have on any panties. She was loving this feeling, but she didn't want the world to know about her new discovery, although she would eventually let Trevor in on her little secret.

Speaking of Trevor, she could hear him making his way to the bedroom to get dressed, as they would be leaving shortly.

"Oh, you're dressed already?" Trevor asked.

"Yep," Whitney replied. "I knew we'd be pushing it to be out of here on time so I got a jumpstart."

"Well, you look lovely as always," Trevor stated, still with the same look in his eyes as the day they met.

"Thank you." Whitney gave him a subtle smile, almost flirtatious in her approach.

"You know that look will get you into trouble, young lady," Trevor said.

"I know, I know. But right now we have a picnic to get to." Whitney walked down the hall to the front room to wait for Trevor.

Trevor loved the way Whitney looked and he really loved that dress. Of course, he hated missing her getting dressed—he wanted to see what panties she had on. He sat wondering if it was a thong, bikini or even her famous booty shorts. One thing that he did know was that whichever pair she chose, she'd be one sexy lady at that picnic.

"Ready?" Trevor asked, walking into the front room.

"As ready as I'm going to be," Whitney replied.

"OK, great. Let's go!"

And off they went.

On the way to the picnic Trevor couldn't help but ask about the panties. It was killing him. He was still on a mission to determine whether or not panty choices could affect a woman's everyday outcome. How could he not ask the big question? It was a must.

"So, babe," Trevor started. "You know I always ask you about your panties, right? Well, I was wondering ... which ones do you have on today? I love, love, love seeing you in them and you are always so unbelievably sexy."

"Is that the only reason you're asking, Trevor?" Whitney asked sternly. "You're just asking because of sex?"

Trevor didn't know what to say at first. He was taken completely off guard and couldn't understand why she seemed so upset.

"What?" Trevor asked. "Sex? I don't know why you're saying that. I always comment about your panties because I think you're sexy, yes, but you're also smart, kind, loving and, in case you forgot, you're my wife."

"Obviously, Trevor," she responded. "I know I'm you're wife. But why the sudden interest in my panties? Before, you would just mention them from time to time, or specify a certain pair that you liked. In some cases they would be brought up if we were going to have sex. But now it's all of the time. Plus, you ask more intently about my day, how I'm feeling, how things went at work—"

"Is that a bad thing?"

"I guess not, but I'm not used to the attention," she explained. "It's like you're just overbearing with it sometimes. Things were fine with us before, but now I feel like you're always in my space about my panties. Sometimes I just like to put them on and go about my day without the 'whys' of it all."

Trevor thought for a moment, wondering if he should reveal his theory and let her in on what he'd been noticing and also what his friends had concluded with their own wives. If he did tell her, would she take it OK, or would she be even more upset? Sometimes women could be so challenging. He wanted to explain his theories because he truly felt that there was something to this panty thing and that, in the end, it could help both of them in more ways than one. But was it too early for the big reveal?

After a few moments, which seemed like an eternity to Whitney, Trevor decided to wait. However, he was going to have to act quickly to ease the tension between the two of them before they arrived at the picnic. One thing he did know was that no matter what, this picnic meant a lot to Whitney. He wanted to make sure she had a good time.

"I'm sorry, Whitney," he started, "I didn't mean anything by it at all. I guess I'm just seeing your panties in a new light. That's it. Nothing more. Maybe all of these years I just saw them as a piece of your clothing and something for special occasions, but now it's different. They are beautiful, no matter what type you're wearing, and I love seeing you in them."

Well, that was a good save! He was proud of the way he handled it. He needed to do whatever was necessary to keep the conversation light so they could enjoy the day ahead.

"In fact," he started again, "what type do you have on today? I can't wait to see them."

Whitney shot him a quick look and said, "I guess you'll have to guess, Mr. Panty Man. If you're right, maybe there'll be a surprise for you this evening." She gave a little wink in his direction. "But if you're wrong, no surprise."

As they pulled into the parking lot, Trevor was thinking about what she could possibly be wearing—but Whitney just knew that he'd never think that she'd go commando.

They grabbed their things out of the trunk and started heading toward the festivities when Trevor shared his "guess work."

"I've got it," he exclaimed.

"OK. Let me hear it," Whitney replied.

"Bikinis?" he asked.

No response.

"A thong?" he asked again.

No response.

"Booty shorts?" Now with more conviction.

Still no response.

"Babe, tell me," he begged.

"I thought you knew so much, Trevor?" Whitney replied.

"That's not fair," Trevor said, getting a bit more frustrated.

"You'll never guess."

She was indeed having fun with this now.

"OK, I give," he conceded.

"Commando," she replied and burst out laughing. "Now you'll get no surprise tonight." She hurried ahead to the picnic area.

Who is this woman I married? Trevor thought to himself, half serious and half joking. *Commando? Really? It doesn't even seem legal. One thing I do know is that I love this woman and I'm learning more and more about her each day.*

* * *

German-American film and theatre director, producer, actor and comedian, Mike Nichols, was present at the celebration in 1962 when Marilyn Monroe famously serenaded then-President John Kennedy on his forty-fifth birthday. This is what he had to say about the experience:

"I was standing right behind Marilyn, completely invisible, when she sang 'Happy birthday, Mr. President,'" Nichols stated. *"And indeed, the corny thing happened: Her dress split for my benefit, and there was Marilyn, and yes, indeed, she didn't wear any underwear."*

"I love commando. I feel free. I especially go this route in the summer when it's hot and I'm wearing a nice full skirt that is loose and flowy. If I wear panties, they are nude in color and are granny panties because then it still looks like I'm wearing nothing at all."
~ Anonymous

"Personally, I don't go commando all the time. It's only when I'm out with my boyfriend and I want to be a little dirty. I say, 'Guess what? I'm not wearing any panties.' It gets him every time." ~ Chelsea W.

* * *

The interest in panties and their allure in the twentieth century has created a multi-billion dollar industry. As a consumer, we want the pretty, the lacy, the colorful and the sexy. And, on occasion, we do look for comfort. Imagine if all women decided to change their style and go *au naturel*? There would be a big dent put in the bottom line of lingerie companies throughout the world.

From the late 1800s to the early 1900s, women often wore heavy petticoats to keep the cold air from blowing up their dresses because the use of underwear was not practiced. It was considered improper for a woman to have anything between her legs, which was also the reason women never wore pants. It was felt that any type of fabric covering an area that was moist would lead to infection, itching and even odor.

As time went on, the term "going commando" was introduced and has since had many derivatives over the years. It originally came from the military meaning "to go without underwear," as we also reference it today, because commandos who would often go without underwear due to harsh environments and to avoid potentially being stuck with wet underwear leading to many medical issues.

As time moved on, the term then became more widely used in the 1980s when college students took hold of it. It even made an appearance on the big screen, when it was first used in an episode of *Friends* in 1994 in which Joey tells his friends that he will not "go commando in another man's fatigues."

Although the perception of how panties are worn has changed over the years, one fact that has remained constant is that for approximately 25% of all women, *going commando* is their number one choice, whether regularly or on occasion. Whether their reasoning comes from a place of hygiene or one of sex appeal and the "no panty line" philosophy, going commando is here to stay—

it is even currently growing in popularity among younger to middle-aged women.

For Whitney, the concept of "going commando" was new and a bit unnerving. Nonetheless, she was seeking to explore all there was to panties—or all there wasn't, if that turned out to be the case—and to embrace the emotions felt with each style worn. Surprisingly, she found that the "pantiless" approach was not as bad as what she had originally thought. It came with a sense of freedom, mystique and a calming element. She felt as though there was nothing between what she wanted and what she could get. Could this be psychologically driven, a connection to the fact that there was nothing between her legs? Maybe so. In either case, going commando was working for her.

Trevor was also taking notice as to the change he was seeing.

Action Items

Ladies

1. If going commando is not your usual style, try it for one week and see what you think. Write down the results. When the time is right, share them with your partner.

2. What myths about going commando did you find to be true and which ones were false?

3. Have some fun with this style and dress up in your best fatigues outfit (which you may have to put together from a thrift store or military surplus shop)—of course while going commando—and waltz around the house in front of your boyfriend or husband. He may know exactly what you're doing; then again, he may need some prompting. Have fun. Be sexy. Be spontaneous. Tell him you're his commander going commando. It may seem awkward and even unnerving if it's not your regular playful personality. But in the end he'll love this new "take-charge" approach and will look forward to more playful nights of going commando.

Gentlemen

1. Get smart on the actual benefits of going commando. If your wife or girlfriend doesn't normally go without panties, make the suggestion to her that you think it would be great if she tried it (but do this *after* you do your research). Have in hand the benefits of it being hygienically sound, without panty lines, extremely sexy (which of course is all about you) and just plain ol' comfortable. She'll be impressed that you actually did some research and didn't just mention it for your own gain.

2. Have a "going commando" day when you both choose to go without. It'll create a bond. Make sure you both share how you feel about the experience. If it just makes you want to have sex more, then find a way to throw in some other "feel good" points too. You'll have some fun with this.

3. Take notice as to how your wife or girlfriend acts when she's in her *au naturel* mode. Is she more fun and spontaneous? Is she more relaxed? Secure? Whatever the changes may be, no matter how vast or subtle, take note of it and share your observations with her at the appropriate time. This may be a way to better connect with her during her "commando" days. Make the suggestion yourself of going commando if

you know this style will benefit her in some way based on her plans for the day.

Period Panties—
Embrace the Flow

The weekend had been great and Whitney and Trevor had a ball at the picnic. They had played games, danced to some of their favorite songs, ate some great BBQ and enjoyed hanging out with fellow colleagues who had become great friends over the years. The turnout was fantastic, too, with over 300 employees and their families in attendance enjoying a day packed with fun.

Although the picnic was filled with good times, Trevor had a difficult time focusing fully on anything other than Whitney's big "commando" reveal. He was so blown away with her decision that he would lose focus in conversations (not to mention while playing games). Plus, the thought of her, his beautiful and sexy wife, walking around all day with no panties was a huge turn-on—and he had no doubt that she knew it, too. But for the most part, he was watching her to see if she was any different as opposed to the times when she was wearing panties. It seemed to him that Whitney was the same, although she was a bit more conscientious about how she carried herself and her movements. She was certainly not as carefree as she usually was.

Whitney, too, found herself to be side tracked every time she felt a cool breeze finding its way up her white and red dress. She had never been so bold—at least not publicly—but she was finding that a part of her enjoyed this feeling of freedom and of being in complete control of herself in a freeing type of way. The other side of her wasn't 100% sold on whether going commando was really all that it was cracked up to be—at least for her, anyway. She'd have to give it a bit more time before she could really make a decision about this new adventure.

"I sure enjoyed the picnic yesterday," Trevor said as the two of them were cleaning up the morning breakfast dishes.

"I agree," Whitney replied. "I think there were more people there this year than last. It seems like it gets better each year. I don't know how they'll top off this year, though. That band was awesome!"

"How well I know," Trevor chuckled. "I thought you'd never come off the dance floor."

"You were out there, too, remember?"

"Of course I do. I was out there with my Commando Wife." He pulled her toward him, greeting her with a kiss.

Whitney passionately responded in kind, lips locked as though they had just begun dating.

"You still know how to give me goosebumps, mister," Whitney said.

"And visa versa, my dear," Trevor responded. "Let's finish up these dishes so we can just relax and enjoy the rest of this day before Monday morning is staring us in the face."

"Sounds great," Whitney said, and kissed him again.

Upon finishing up the kitchen, Whitney decided she would take a shower. She was eager to spend the day relaxing with Trevor, perhaps watching some movies. In fact, they had been planning a *Godfather* weekend, watching all four movies from start to finish, and today was going to be the perfect day for that.

"I thought we could do our *Godfather* day today, babe," Whitney suggested.

"Oh, yeah, I had forgotten about that," Trevor replied. "That's a great idea."

"OK, I'm going to take a quick shower and then I'll be ready," Whitney said.

"I'll be here," Trevor replied with a smirk and a look in his eye that would make any girl go crazy.

"Are you serious?" Whitney called out from the bathroom.

Trevor could tell something was wrong due to the frustration in her voice.

"What's wrong?" he asked.

"My period started," she replied. "Good ol' Aunt Flow. I'm so mad!"

Trevor sat on the edge of the bed where he had been taking off his shoes, also getting ready to hit the shower once Whitney was done. He was quiet. He didn't know what to say.

Why today? he thought to himself.

"Hello?" Whitney yelled.

"I'm here, honey," Trevor responded. "It'll be fine. Don't worry about it."

"Of course it will be ... in five days!" Whitney yelled back, now a bit more frustrated.

Whitney always seemed to be a bit of a handful during her monthly cycle. Sometimes she'd be fine and then two minutes later she was irritated and didn't want to be bothered in any form or fashion. And it was looking like it was going to be the same way this go-around. You would think that after four years of marriage, Trevor would "embrace the flow" and have a better handle on this period thing, but it was apparent that he still had a lot to learn.

As he waited for Whitney to finish up, he pulled out the movies and put the first one in the DVD player so it'd be ready to go.

"Well, you look nice and fresh," Trevor said to Whitney as she entered the room.

Silence.

"I got the movies out. I'm glad you brought it up again. It'll be fun," he added.

Silence.

"Come on, babe," he said, trying to get her to relax. "I can rub your feet or something while we watch the movie if that'll make you feel better."

Finally Whitney came to her senses and said a few words.

"I know, and I appreciate you being so helpful," Whitney replied. "I just hate periods. I hate not feeling good."

Trevor decided not to say anything more and just wait to see where things would go.

Whitney walked over to her dresser, pulled out her panty drawer and began rummaging around toward the back. Trevor continued sitting quietly, wondering what she was doing and what kind of panties she was going to put on. It seemed that she was looking forever, until finally, there they were. A pair of dark blue granny panties with small yellow duckies all over them.

What in the heck are those? Trevor thought to himself. *I never even knew she owned something with ducks on them.*

These panties had been around for a while, no doubt. But they were still in decent shape and obviously something that Whitney liked.

Trevor couldn't keep it to himself any longer. He had to ask.

"Babe, I've never seen those before. When did you get them?"

"I've had these for a while," she replied. "These are my period panties. I have a green pair with puppies on them, I have a pink pair with panda bears on them and I also have a black pair with lavender butterflies all over. Plus these."

"You have period panties?" Trevor asked. "Like panties you wear just for your period?"

"Yes, Trevor," she said, clearly annoyed with the questions. "What's the problem? You seem weirded out."

"Not really," he replied. "I just didn't know you had some designated for *that*. Do all women have 'period panties'?"

"I don't know. Some do for sure. It's just easier that way. Then you don't mess up your pretty ones. Plus, I have ones that are cute because they just make me feel better when I don't feel well."

Trevor sat pondering this whole new "period panties" thing. He thought he was getting it all figured out, but then this came along and threw a wrench in everything. He was definitely going to have to talk with his friends about this one and see what they knew about period panties, if anything.

In the meantime, Whitney finished getting dressed, period panties and all. She did look cute in her little yellow ducky skivvies. She proceeded to the medicine cabinet, grabbed some pain relievers and headed to the kitchen for a cup of coffee.

"Do you want anything from the kitchen?" she asked Trevor.

"Sure, I'll take a cup of coffee too. Thanks!"

When she returned, Trevor had the movie going and, to her surprise, some lotion in hand.

"Put the coffee down and come over her so I can massage your feet, just like I said I would," he said, smiling.

"You don't have to, but if you insist ..." She stretched out, smiling back, and placed her feet next to him within easy reach.

Trevor was going to keep figuring this panty thing out, period panties and all.

He grabbed the remote and hit "play," and their *Godfather* marathon began.

"Thanks for not getting completely weirded out by my period panties," Whitney said. "I know some guys just can't take it, like women don't have periods or something."

"I definitely don't want to be one of *those* guys," Trevor replied. "I just didn't know you had panties dedicated to the monthly fun."

The two of them sat back and enjoyed the rest of the weekend. But in the back of Trevor's mind, he couldn't wait to talk to his friends the following weekend.

* * *

"My stay-at-home period panties are Elmo/Cookie Monster panties."
~ Anonymous

"There's nothing better than a good book, some hot chocolate, a heating pad and your favorite period panties." ~ Anonymous

"I remember this time when my boyfriend was over and we were doing laundry together. He had pulled the clothes out of the dryer and found this very ragged pair of panties that looked like they were on their last leg (but not mine, hee hee). He held them up with two fingers and asked what these things were. I proudly said, 'They're my period panties.' I literally thought he was going to throw up on the spot. I told him they were clean and to get over it. He just threw them at me and then wiped his hands on the floor like there was some fungus growing on them. It was the funniest thing ever, but men just need to understand that every woman has her period panties and loves them, whether she admits it or not." ~ *Anonymous*

* * *

Period panties have either been a woman's best kept secret or men have never wanted to embrace the topic of periods, keeping the subject a mystery never to be solved. Trevor was no different. He was still perplexed about Whitney and her period panties. Could he have been so blind and not realized that there were certain panties that went with certain times of the month? It was hard for him to believe that he'd been missing this for the past four years—or, like a lot of men, maybe he just wasn't paying attention.

But now there's a "new" Trevor in town. He would learn as much as he could about Whitney and her panties—and of course he would consult the guys, too. If he wanted to understand the way a woman feels when she wears certain types of panties, then period panties had to be a part of that equation.

We can unequivocally say that the styles of panties have changed over the years. I'm sure that in another twenty years there will be new trends of panties available to those future generations. However, the one thing that will never change is the fact that women have periods. Eighty percent of all women own period panties. The styles used for those period panties may differ, but the basic use of those exclusive skivvies remains the same.

Most men have a tough time dealing with their lady's monthly splendor. Most completely despise going to the store to pick up needed supplies. So when you start talking with them about period panties, they begin to convulse, quiver and some even heave. Aren't panties supposed to be something sexy? Something for those special nights rolling around in the hay? How can these little treasures of joy even be used in the same sentence as period panties? It just doesn't feel right.

Well, gentlemen, with 80% of women claiming to own and use period panties, the subject isn't going away. It's here to stay. The best advice I can offer is to simply *embrace the flow*. Give your woman whatever she needs to get through those few days and be supportive. If it's period panties that she needs, then don't be a scrooge. Understand that it is just part of the process.

One thing new to the scene, however, is Thinx, the ultimate period panty. They have been designed to eliminate pads and tampons (or any other type of period remedy you may use) through the use of these panties. If you use these, then you don't need anything else. They come in three styles: Hiphugger (for the heaviest days), Hi-Waist (for the medium days) and the Thong (for the light days). They can be washed and worn month after month until you choose to throw them away. They are a great way to usher in the flow and take period panties to a whole new level.

Action Items

Ladies

1. **Pamper yourself!** As you're well aware, your period is not going anywhere anytime soon. So start some monthly traditions that help you get through the time. Maybe it's having your own movie day, or simply doing nothing—meaning no chores, cooking, dishes, etc. Let it be your day. Your significant other will understand once you explain it to him. You could even take the time to catch up on the book you've been wanting to read.

2. **Everyone loves a new pair of period panties.** Each month, purchase a new pair of period panties and add them to your monthly collection. Let them be the ones that make you feel pampered, relaxed and are soothing to the monthly blues. Every woman loves new panties, no matter what the style. So this way you'll be getting at least one pair a month that will be your friend during the tough times.

3. **Think Thinx!** If you haven't already, make it a point to try the new period panties, Thinx. They are indeed something different, but surprisingly, they do work and work better than you'd think. They may take your period collection to another level.

Gentlemen

1. **What makes her tick?** You know your wife or girlfriend better than anyone (at least I hope so). You know what food she likes. You know what styles of clothing she likes and the music she listens to. You know what she likes to read and what movies she likes to watch. So think of one thing (and it doesn't have to break the bank, either) that you can do for her or give her once a month to help her through her period. Maybe it's getting her the new movie she's been waiting for or a Starbucks to start her morning. You're smart and you're insightful. You can make a huge difference by showing her that you care.

2. **Expect nothing.** When I say "Expect nothing," I mean *nothing*. Give her a break. Let her get through these few days in peace. If she's not feeling well, order dinner in and sit on the couch, watch TV and eating Chinese. If you do that, then you'll have no dishes to do either. A win-win! Help out where you can. Pick up the kids if necessary and offer to make her some hot chocolate (but only if she likes that, of course). She will relish the fact that you care and understand how she's feeling, especially when you're making it all about her and expecting nothing in return.

3. **Buy her some new period panties.** If you're looking for some big bonus points from your honey, buy her a

pair of period panties. First off, make sure that you've taken the time to see what type of period panties she wears and then purchase something along those lines. In other words, if she wears granny panties as her period undies, don't go and buy her a G-string. Let her know that you've noticed the types of period panties she's been wearing and you wanted to buy her something new. She will be shocked. You can even put them in a cute box with a card and some chocolate. That'll really score some extra points.

Also, you can check out the Build a Cycle Set at Thinx and design a set of different types of period panties for her. If you're not quite sure, just call their customer service number and there will be a happy voice on the other end that will guide you through the process.

Ain't Nothin' But a G-String

"I was thinking I'd pick up the snacks for you to take to over to Justin's tonight," said Whitney. "Are all of the guys going to be there?"

"Oh, that's great, honey," replied Trevor. "And yes, I believe they'll all be there, at least that's the last I heard."

"OK. Then I'll make sure I get enough snacks. You guys really know how to eat when you're playing cards."

"Very true," Trevor said with a soft laugh. "Very true. Do you have any plans tonight?"

"Well, it *is* Friday night," she laughed, "but no, not really. I think I'm just going to enjoy a quiet night cuddling up to that book I started about a month ago. It'll be nice to have some alone time," she said, winking at Trevor.

"Ha ha ha," Trevor laughed sarcastically. "I understand, but just don't be *too* excited to get alone time."

"Of course not, babe. I'll be right here waiting for you when you get home—well, me and Digger, of course," she joked.

No matter how frustrated Trevor would get at times with Whitney, he knew she was the perfect woman for him and knew that as the years went on, their bond would only continue to strengthen as long as they both put in the effort.

Over the past several days, Trevor had been quite in tune with Whitney. He'd noticed how she was feeling during her monthly cycle. He wanted to be supportive and caring, and he wanted to take in all that he could regarding his new understanding of period panties so he could learn just a little more about his theory.

Trevor focused on being kind and understanding and even fixed Whitney her nightly dose of hot chocolate with marshmallows. He noticed it seemed to soften her mood while also helping her feel better. He was certainly paying more attention than he had in the past. Now he definitely recognized the differences between Whitney's regular panties versus her period panties. It seemed that she liked to wear the ones that were just cute, not sexy, and those that made her feel comfortable and secure. The odd thing about this revelation was that although she was just going after "cute," somehow Trevor found these choices to be sexy, too.

Was it that he was seeing his wife in her entirety, inside and out? Was he just now taking the time to see what makes her tick, to understand her, and to explore the characteristics that made her who she was? One thing Trevor did notice was that through him simply being considerate and thoughtful about how Whitney was feeling, he found that she responded in kind. They argued much less, their conversations were more light and fun and even when there were serious matters to discuss, the conversations seemed to flow with ease.

"OK, babe. I'll see you after work. I'll have the snacks for you." Whitney stated leaning in to give Trevor a kiss goodbye.

"Thanks, sweetie," he replied. "I appreciate it ... and you."

"I know." She gave her flirtatious giggle that always brought a smile to Trevor's face. "Also, I'm meeting up with Bree, Sophia and Lisa today for lunch. We're going to that Italian place, Carminos, on 15th Street."

"Sounds like fun," he replied. "Tell them I said hello."

"OK. Gotta go. Love you."

"Love you, too," he echoed.

Carminos was packed. It seemed everyone from the city was having lunch.

"I thought I'd never find a parking space," Bree said as she approached her friends waiting to be seated.

"I know," Lisa responded. "I circled around forever."

"Me too," Sophia chimed in.

"At least we have a reservation," Whitney said. "They should be calling us shortly."

As always, the food was great. Carminos had been around for over 30 years and everyone flocked to it on a daily basis. No other Italian restaurant ever offered a free complimentary glass of wine with any entrée, and that certainly made for a great draw.

"I just love this place," Lisa said.

"Not to mention the wine," Sophia added.

"I'm just glad to be having lunch with my besties," Bree said.

Everyone laughed and agreed in unison, toasting to their lifelong friendship.

"So has anyone been noticing anything weird about the panties and our husbands since the last time we talked about it at the dog park?" Lisa asked.

Everyone started nodding "yes" in agreement.

"I can definitely say it's been a major topic, whether spoken or not, in our house," Whitney responded.

"Really?" asked Bree. "In what way?"

"Mine too, actually," Sophia quickly added.

"Let me ask you guys something," Whitney began. "Do you guys wear period panties?"

"Duh," Lisa said. "Doesn't everyone?"

"I'm sure everyone does," Bree added.

"It seems that Trevor never noticed that I have period panties—certainly not like he does now," Whitney said. "Like I told you guys before, he pays attention to everything. During my period earlier this week, not only did he say he found my cutesy period panties 'sexy,' but he was bringing me hot chocolate in bed each night and massaging my feet."

"Wow," Lisa said.

"I'd give anything for Brenton to do that," Sophia added.

"Me too," said Bree.

"I must admit, it's been nice," Whitney replied.

"I know that after we met at the dog park, I noticed that Justin was more interested in my panties. Asking me why I picked out certain ones," Bree said. "You guys know how I am. I hate anyone in my space, but because we were trying to figure this thing out with our husbands, I entertained his inquiries."

"So what did you do?" Sophia asked.

"I answered his questions," Bree said, slightly annoyed. "I told him how I was feeling, why I wore certain pairs and how they made me feel."

"That's deep," Lisa said.

"I wanted to be honest to see where this was gonna go," Bree continued. "And what I found was that he was genuinely interested, and the more I told him, the more I noticed him becoming in tune with me and with us as a couple over the days that followed."

"Why do you think there's been such a change in his interest?" Whitney asked.

"I guess that there must have been some type of conversation he had with the guys at some point about bikinis and that they seem to make one's mood more relaxed, self assured and amenable."

Everyone started laughing.

"You? Amenable?" Lisa asked.

Again, everyone giggled.

"I guess so," Bree replied, "because that's what Justin said. So I told myself I'd try it. I'd focus on carrying these traits with me throughout the day while I was wearing bikini panties, and who would've thought ... it worked! I was more confident. Less apt to get frustrated when things didn't go according to plan, more relaxed in conversations with Justin as we planned out different things."

"As surprised as I am," Whitney said, "I think Trevor is on to something."

"I think so, too," Lisa agreed.

"You guys know they are meeting at my house tonight, right?" Bree asked.

Everyone nodded their heads in agreement.

"I can't wait to hear the latest out of that meet-up," Lisa said.

"Well, I'll have a surprise waiting for Trevor when he gets home tonight," Whitney said.

"What?" Sophia asked.

"I told him I'll be reading my book, which I will be," Whitney explained. "But when he comes in the bedroom I'll be on the bed in my nice robe, of course reading my book ... and with nothing on underneath but a G-string."

"Oh, my goodness!" Lisa exclaimed. "He's going to go crazy."

"Yeah," Bree added. "More crazy for you."

"He deserves it," Whitney said. "He's been so caring and thoughtful. I want to do what I can to make things good from my end, too. It's a two-way street."

"I totally agree," Sophia nodded. "In fact, I might have to see what I can come up with tonight myself."

"We should all do it," Lisa said excitedly.

"For sure," Bree added. "We'll all do the G-string thing."

"Sounds like a plan," Whitney said.

It seemed that Justin was killing everyone at cards. He had more "money" in front of him than anyone else, without a doubt. They were really only playing for chips, but the ultimate loser would be responsible for bringing the snacks at the next card night. And Trevor didn't want to have to bring snacks twice in a row.

"How can you take advantage of us in your own house?" Harrison asked.

"You can always host the next get-together at your house, Harrison," Justin responded, chuckling. "Then maybe you'll win."

"Oooh," Trevor said.

"You're not going to take that, are you, Harrison?" Brenton asked.

Everyone laughed and ate the remainder of the snacks that Trevor had brought.

"Better yet," Justin said, "why not have it at your house, Trevor? I'm sure Whitney would be thrilled to have us all there for the evening, but at least you'd have a shot at winning, being on your own turf and all."

"You definitely have jokes, Justin," Trevor said, "but, you know, it's not a bad idea. Whitney would love it. In fact, she seems OK with practically everything these days, and when she's not, we discuss it and work through it."

"Wow. Nice," Brenton responded.

"It really is," Trevor nodded. "I don't know how you guys have been doing with the panty thing and trying to gain more insight into the panties—other than the obvious," and they all laughed, "but it's really made a difference for Whitney and me."

"I have to agree," Harrison responded. "I know there was this day that I had commented on a thong that Lisa was going to put on. It was *very* nice. But then she put it back and, to my surprise, pulled up the skirt that she was going to wear and walked out of the room with no panties. I was standing in awe thinking, 'Did she really just do that?' So I followed her into the kitchen and asked her if she was really going to go out with no panties. She gave me her 'Lisa look' that takes me to oh-so many great places and said, 'Yes I am. I like it like that sometimes. The possibilities in life are endless and you never know what might happen.' I had no idea what she was talking about, but I do know what I was thinking."

"So what did you do?" Trevor asked.

"Were you guys going out somewhere together?" Brenton asked.

"Yes. We were on our way to dinner at her parents' house."

"Her parents' house?" Justin said in complete disbelief. "Who goes to their parents' with no panties?"

With a chuckle, Harrison replied, "Lisa. Yep, Lisa. And we had a great time. She was fun, energetic, flirty and holding my hand, and I just rolled with the flow. No pressure. No weird comments. I was not about to ruin a good thing and miss the possibility of an even better evening with some 'dessert.' "

"Well?" Trevor asked. "Did you get 'dessert'?"

"Of course I did," Harrison went on, "but the odd thing about it was that even after the evening was over and the 'dessert' was gone, there was just a stronger bond between us. It was like through all of this panty stuff we've been talking about, I found a place of peace in her—in us. There was no fussing and frustration. I know we are married and everything, but aside from the sex I was finally seeing her as my true best friend. No obstacles, no fears of being completely honest. It was being able to see one another at face value. We had a common goal together and it was through the panties that we were reaching it."

"That's awesome," Brenton responded. "I am beginning to see some of the same things between Sophia and I—even regarding her and her period panties, as crazy as that may sound."

"You too?" Trevor stated. "I just went through that this week with Whitney. I never thought I'd say it, but I totally understand the whole monthly thing better now than I thought I ever would before. I don't really mind it as much now."

"I'm with you," Justin chimed in. "For us, I think I saw a breakthrough with the bikinis. Bree is just another person with those bikinis. I just love it."

"You'd better stock up then," Harrison joked.

"I have to tell you, Trevor," Brenton said, "you have sure opened up my eyes to your panty theory, and it sounds like I'm not alone. I'm really grateful that you shared it with us."

"Me too," Justin agreed. "I have one question, though. We've talked about a lot of panties, but have any of your wives been wearing a G-string?"

Everyone sat contemplating the question. Eventually they each shook their head.

"I guess there's still some more research to be done," Trevor said. "Maybe we can mention it to our wives and see what happens."

"Agreed," they all said.

Trevor got back to the house, glad he hadn't lost the card game and excited to see his wife.

"Hi, honey!" Trevor shouted from the kitchen.

"Hi," Whitney called back. "I'm in bed with my book."

"OK," Trevor responded. "I'll be up in a minute."

After turning out the lights in the front part of the house, Trevor ran upstairs and entered the bedroom. There she was, reading her book and wearing one of his favorite robes of hers. He couldn't help but wonder what was underneath, but chose not to share that thought.

"Did you have a nice time?" she asked.

"Yeah, it was fun. And I didn't lose this time."

Whitney laughed. "At least you won't have to take the snacks next time."

"Very true. In fact, next time we get together we are going to have it here."

"Cool," she responded.

Trevor had known she'd have no problem with it, but he loved that she was so open to it.

"Well ... are you gonna come get in bed?" she asked with anticipation.

"Yep. Let me just get out of these clothes and put these shoes in the closet."

Before he could move too far, Whitney let her robe fall open to one side. He took one look and as fast as he could, he pulled off his clothes and joined her on the bed. As he began to pull the other side of her robe back, he looked down at her panties.

"Is that what I think it is?"

"It *ain't nothin' but a G-string,*" she sang.

Trevor couldn't believe it.

Is this really happening? he thought to himself. *We just talked about this at Justin's house.*

Whitney loved seeing the excitement on Trevor's face. It made her happy. She couldn't help but wonder if her friends were getting the same reaction, since they had all decided to wear a G-string for the night. Only time would tell, but for now, it was back to business.

"I like the look on a guy's face when they see you're wearing a G-string." ~ Anonymous

"I've always been a bikini girl until a few of my friends bought me some undies for my birthday one year. In the package was a G-string. Now my panties collection is 50/50 G-strings and bikinis. I love it!" ~ Anonymous

"All I need is a cup of coffee in the morning and a really cute G-string. The rest will take care of itself." ~ Pam

The G-string dates back to the 1920s, when it was worn by showgirls in stage productions during the period known as the Jazz Age and the Roaring Twenties. When nudity wasn't allowed in certain venues, the G-string would be used as a way of still offering sex appeal without having complete nudity. This risqué undergarment showed off the butt cheeks while covering the groin area—hence the term "G-string."

By the 1930s, the G-string was being worn by major stage performers, especially in burlesque shows in Chicago. To this end, Chicago became the largest manufacturing area for G-strings in the country. During this time, the G-string was used as a tease for onlookers in all types of venues. In fact, dancers would wear layers of G-strings that they could take off during a strip tease, with each one more revealing than the last. As time went on, however, the G-string became the normal costume for topless clubs and was then lost completely at all nude venues.

One thing that still holds true today is that the original intent of the G-string, which was to create sex appeal and promote enticing sexual behavior, has not changed or veered from its inception. However, the G-string is now more widely accepted as regular attire, worn publicly at beaches and pools all over the world. And, of course, you can find plenty of colors and styles in lingerie stores to be used for those special occasions when you want to turn up the heat with your hubby or boyfriend.

For the majority of women who wear a G-string, they also enjoy the commando approach on occasion when getting ready for the day. However, most "commando" girls don't necessarily make this choice if they're wearing pants or shorts and choose a G-string instead. There are still no panty lines to be seen, and the G-string does offer a small amount of fabric between the skin and the clothing.

All in all, the G-string is definitely a must-have for the majority of women when it comes to wanting to look sexy—that added spice on date night with the hubby or boyfriend. Just like the "commando girl," who feels free and that nothing will stand in her way, the "G-string girl" has that same sense of adventure, sexual freedom and boldness.

Let's look at Whitney. She wanted Trevor to feel appreciated. She wanted to show him that she was grateful for the understanding that he had shown her during her monthly cycle and that she was paying attention to how attentive he had become to her needs and in their relationship. She knew that a G-string under a nice silky robe would be all that was needed for an awesome night in bed and her own little way of saying "thank you."

Action Items

Ladies

1. **Let go of the hangups.** If you're thinking that you can't wear a G-string, whatever the reason may be—and as women, we have plenty of excuses—let it go. Nine times out of ten, your husband or boyfriend loves being with you because he loves you. If you think you have too much bulge in the hip area, guess what? He already knows. It's not something he's seeing for the first time. But if you've never been into wearing a G-string before and you suddenly prance into the bedroom, flaws and all, wearing a sexy little piece of fabric (otherwise known as a G-string), you will undoubtedly knock him off his feet, right into the bed and right into a deeper understanding of you and who you are together. So don't miss out on the fun. Take charge and wear that thing!

2. **For his eyes only.** As you're getting ready to leave for work, move about in your regular routine. Maybe it's getting breakfast, or packing the kids' lunches or making the coffee. Whatever it is, stay consistent. Then, just before you're ready to leave for the day, give him a hug and a kiss and encourage his hands to move around to the small of your back, eventually feeling the G-string. If you're wearing a dress, let him feel it through your dress. He will be so excited and

want to see it. Resist the urge. Tell him he will need to wait until later. The curiosity will be with him all day.

3. **The G-string card.** If you know that your husband or boyfriend loves it when you wear a G-string, then give him a "G-string card" on occasion. This is a "freebie" for him to use when he wants you to wear one, and it is good for any occasion. You can be as creative as you want to be with this. You can either buy a card and write something nice in it (i.e. "Thank you for being so caring and such an awesome husband," etc., or "I was thinking about you and how much you mean to me," etc.) *or* just write something cute with some colorful ink on a 3-by-5 card.

Now this is the most important part: make sure that you also write "Redeemable at any time for the complete G-string package." He will go crazy trying to figure out exactly what that means, while you take the opportunity to create your "package" (and ladies, get creative!). In the meantime, let him think about it and let him work to get his first G-string card. This will be tons of fun and a great way to draw the two of you closer together and more in tune with one another.

Gentlemen

1. **The dancing diva.** The G-string has been known to be worn by exotic dancers for many years. So why not bring the dance into your home? Tell your wife you have a special game that you want to play, but she has to wear a G-string (the rest of the outfit is optional). Let her know that you have a surprise for her—and be sincere so she'll believe you. Put on some music that she can dance to, and as she starts dancing put small notecards or pieces of paper in her G-string that have different tasks written on them that you'll do for her. It could be giving her a massage, watching a chick flick together, cooking dinner (or getting some delivered if you don't cook), etc. The more she dances, the more she gets. Make her work for it. Make her feel special and sexy. Cheer her on. She'll love this game, and you'll get all that attention for yourself, too. This will definitely be a win-win for you both.

2. **Don't take the G-string for granted.** Not all women are comfortable in a G-string. Many women, no matter how they look and how many times they've been told they're beautiful, often feel less than perfect. This is your time to shine and make her feel like a movie star. Encourage her. Do some of those "over-the-top" things that she likes, whether in bed or just out and about running errands. And when she puts that G-string on, really let her know how perfect she is

in your eyes. The only thing that matters is how you feel about one another. If your wife or girlfriend doesn't normally wear a G-string, then pick one up for her and encourage her to wear it. If she comes back with comments of not being pretty or she's too fat or too skinny, etc., just tell her she's beautiful and that you can't wait to see her in it.

3. **Ignore the allure of the G-string.** As hard as this may seem, if you see her sauntering around in a G-string, dying for your attention, ignore her. Try to focus on something else. Change the subject. Talk about trivial things. The objective is to throw her off her game. She knows that you normally love to see the G-string, but now you're showing no interest. Keep this going until you can't take it any more (and you'll probably be almost laughing by this time) and then grab her and hold her. Give her the biggest kiss ever. You learned to be patient and she learned to give more to get your attention. This will surely take the romance to a new level.

The End

"I was thinking that we'd go get the wood this afternoon for the shelving you've been wanting for the garage," Whitney said while pouring her morning cup of coffee.

"Oh, yeah?" Trevor asked. He was sitting at the kitchen table enjoying his breakfast. "I thought you said we didn't need shelves in the garage."

"I know, but I was thinking about your idea more. It would make sense and give us more room for some things—your tools, too."

Trevor was lost. He couldn't help but wonder why the change of heart. Whitney had been adamant about not wanting the shelves and said they would be just another place to store junk.

"Well, all righty then," he said. "Sounds like a plan, hon. I do have to ask though, why the sudden change of heart? You were definite about not wanting the shelves before."

"I know. I was being selfish for whatever reason and when I stopped and thought about it, it was a good idea. I don't know why I didn't see that from the start."

Whitney paused for a moment to pull up a chair at the table and mull over what she was about to say.

"It seems that as of late, you've been different," she started. "You've been much more caring and thoughtful, listening to my thoughts and concerns. You've taken the time to understand how I was feeling and haven't been so quick to get upset with me. It's been awesome, but weird, if that makes any sense."

"It definitely does, and I understand," Trevor responded. "It's been odd in a way for me too, and I've enjoyed getting to know you ... again."

"I'm not sure what that means exactly, but if I had to guess, I would say you're referring to your sudden interest in my panty collection?"

"Yes. I definitely am."

"There has certainly been a change in you as you've been 'discovering' new things. As much as I hate to admit it, you might be the smartest person I know," she said with a slight giggle.

"*Might* be?"

"You know what I mean," she laughed. "Remember that day when we found my lavender bikinis out in the garage?"

"I sure do."

"That's when it all started," she said. "You changed that day. I don't know why or how, but you began to see me differently. From what I could tell, it was from my panties. I don't know how you've done it, but it sure has been working. It's like that day of 'walking down memory lane' opened up an entirely new aspect of our relationship. You've always loved me, I know that, but now it's like it's not just about you loving me anymore. It's as though you can read my mind. You know how I feel and what is important to me, sometimes better than I know for myself. You've truly become my best friend. Everything is just ... easy between us. It doesn't matter how I'm feeling, you always seem to understand. You make suggestions to how my day will go, or should go, and then pair my panties with it for the best outcome. It's just ... crazy! I'm really trying to understand it all. I mean, are you psychic or something?"

They both laughed.

"I know I married a smart man. That is evident. But I must say that you've taught me a lot over these past couple of months, and for that, I'm grateful."

"Wow, babe," Trevor said, pausing to take in all that Whitney had just said. "I'm glad you feel like you do about all this panty stuff, because, truthfully, I had no idea my theory would turn out like it has and actually show some positive results. I'm just really happy it did, for both of us. I always saw panties as something nice for a guy to look at, but never really understood anything more than that."

"Actually, I never really did either," Whitney admitted.

"The day when you found those lavender bikinis was an eye opener for me. You were so excited. And then when you put them on, you were just this free person, loving life, laughing and having fun. I couldn't help but wonder if there were some magic in those panties, beyond what I already know, of course."

Whitney laughed again. "Trevor, you are so crazy."

"I know," he said, "but it's true."

Trevor took a deep breath to continue sharing his thoughts and, ultimately, his findings.

"So when I realized how important those bikinis were to you, I decided to do some research of my own. I began first looking at the types of panties you wore and tried to see if you wore them at certain times. In other words, I wanted to know if you wore different styles when you were going out with the girls or when you had a big event at the office or even when we were going out for the evening. If so, I wanted to know how those panties would make you feel as opposed to a different style."

"I can't believe you've put so much thought into all of this, babe," Whitney interjected.

"I wanted to know, hon."

Trevor continued.

"After I gathered some facts, I did some of my own research in books and on the Internet. I even talked to the guys about it."

"Yeah, I figured that out when I talked to the girls one day while we were at the dog park," Whitney said.

"The guys thought I was crazy at first and felt uncomfortable talking to me about the panties their wives wore, which I completely understood."

"Yeah, I would think that's weird too," Whitney added.

"But after they heard me out, they decided to start looking into it themselves. The biggest indicator was when Justin realized that Bree was a lot easier to deal with and willing to make spur-of-the-moment decisions when she was wearing bikini panties. He was sold after that."

"That's so funny," Whitney responded. "We all actually talked about that at lunch the other day, because everybody knows how Bree can be. So that was definitely a good test."

"So as I continued doing my investigative work," Trevor continued with a sly and secretive voice, "I thought I had it all figured out—but then you threw me a curve ball."

"I did?" Whitney asked.

"Yes, you did," Trevor said, smiling. "It was the period panties."

Whitney laughed.

"I mean it! It had me baffled," he continued. "I had figured everything out—or so I thought—but I soon realized that in all the years I'd known you, I never noticed that you had period panties. It was just crazy to me ... and then I had to admit to myself that I guess I hadn't paid attention to certain things about you as much as I had thought. That was a real eye opener to me and something that I wanted to fix."

Whitney sat quietly, listening intently.

"I felt I had 'cracked the panty code' up to that point," he said.

"You mean up until the period panties?" Whitney asked.

"Yeah. I wanted to prove my panty theory, maybe even share it with other guys at some point to help them understand their own wife or girlfriend, but most importantly, I wanted to strengthen my relationship with you."

Whitney was speechless. She had always known that Trevor was a great husband, but her level of admiration for him had just jumped off the charts. She was truly moved by his care, compassion and concern for her and their marriage.

"You definitely 'cracked the panty code,' as you say," Whitney replied. "I couldn't be any more pleased or feel any more special than I do right now, and for that I thank you. Aside from us, I really do feel that you should share your theory. It's proven to work. Bree, Sophia and Lisa have all said that they've seen a difference in their husbands—they've even learned a bit more about themselves through all of this. In fact, Sophia told me the other day that she's found a new love for wearing a thong.

She said it boosts her confidence. She even went so far as to say that she's going to speak to her boss about a new position she wants to get in the company."

"Wow. That's awesome," Trevor said. "That's a big step for her. She's usually so timid at work."

"I know, that's why I think you need to tell people about all that you've been doing. If it can help all of us, I'm sure it can help others, too."

Trevor sat in silence, thinking about what Whitney had said.

"You're right, Whitney," he said with sincerity and excitement. "Maybe that's what this whole experiment was all about: helping people, starting with us. And if that's the case, that would be amazing."

"I guess you'd better get to doing some more research and find a bunch of people to help," she said with a coy smile. "I'm going to get ready so we can go get the stuff you need for those shelves."

"Oh, are you now?" Trevor replied.

"Yep." She stood up from the table.

"Well, I have one question for you, my lovely lady," Trevor said playfully.

"What's that?"

"What kind of panties will you be wearing today?"

Whitney laughed again.

"Which ones do you think, Mr. Private Investigator?" she answered.

"Based on the fact that you've had a change of heart about the shelves and you seem to be so excited to be a part of the project—and agreeable, too—I'd have to say ... booty shorts."

"Wow. You are good. I guess you've thoroughly done your homework."

Trevor walked across the room and gave his wife a kiss, to which she willingly responded.

"Now let's get going," Trevor said. "We've got shelves to build."

* * *

"I once grabbed a jacket from the clean laundry pile and ran to an early work shift at 4:30 a.m. I work as a personal trainer and I trained my first client at the time. Halfway through the session, I saw that a Velcro zipper on my jacket's back had a lacy thong attached to it, which was flapping merrily from my back." ~ Vivi S.

"I love the panties my husband passionately pulled off when we first ever made love, which have ever since been special to me (although they are very old now!). They are pink and make me feel good!!!" ~ Anonymous

"In high school I made up a panty recycling business for a class and cut and sewed panties together ... hehe!" ~ Shelli

"I was elated the day I discovered the Lacie panty from Victoria's Secret. I can't stand panty lines but I also need comfort and these stretch. You would have thought I had found the holy grail!" ~ Dee

* * *

As Trevor stated, most men think of panties in a way that is self-serving and something nice to look at. However, to his surprise, he saw something different. He saw an opportunity to use panties in a way that would normally be of no meaningful importance, one that would strengthen his relationship. He was insightful and ventured down a path never before traveled. Not only did he take the time to understand his wife, but he also shared the information with "the guys," which most men would be reluctant to do.

Just as Trevor has done, "understanding the psyche of a woman, one panty at a time" is something anyone can do, and it can be a journey that is fun, adventurous and enlightening. If you're a man reading this book, don't be afraid to ask the tough questions about your wife or girlfriend's panty choices. Ask her why or why not. Ask about the dreaded period panties (and then stop dreading them!). Ask how she feels wearing certain styles. If you're a woman reading this, ask yourself these same questions—because whether you're in a relationship or not, understanding yourself is the first step to any form of success, personal or professional.

The one thing that will never change about panties is their necessity. As we've seen, the styles of underwear have changed significantly over the years and women today have more choices than ever before. With more choices come more opportunities. Undoubtedly, panties will continue to evolve from generation to generation, but the one aspect that will remain constant is their uniqueness and significance to the women wearing them.

Action Items

Ladies

1. **Find your panty superpower!** Are you adventurous, charming, outgoing, loving, independent or imaginative? Or, are there other characteristics that you possess? Pick one that relates most to your favorite panty style and strengthen that superpower. Let it lead you to a new and exciting place in your life and give you what you are missing. You may find that each style of panty has its own superpower, which will empower you to choose your panties wisely depending on the desired outcome.

2. **Create a panty ritual.** Pick your favorite pair of panties. It doesn't matter the style or the color. Then choose a ritual for yourself when these undies are worn (or not worn if you're going commando). Maybe it's wearing black pants or wearing a certain perfume or knowing you'll relax in a nice bubble bath after a day at work. Or, better yet, maybe the ritual is with your significant other. It could be ten kisses after you put those beauties on or simply leaving a love note on the front seat of his car before he leaves for work. The goal is to have fun with this. When you get bored with one ritual, change it up to a different one!

3. **Panty pics.** If you know that you're wearing your favorite panties, then your significant other probably does, too. So why not share the day with him? As you go throughout your day, take some pics of what your panties are up to. You can either take actual shots of your panties wherever you may be or you can just take selfies of yourself at different locations. In either case, your panties are out and about having a good day and it will certainly peak his curiosity.

Gentlemen

1. **Create your own panty ritual.** If you see that your wife or girlfriend is wearing *your* favorite panties, then have a ritual of something that you do for her. Maybe it's making dinner or breakfast. Perhaps it's doing the shopping for the day or even a nice foot massage after a long day. Your reward is those unbelievably adorable panties. So why not make it just as special for her?

2. **Put together a Panty Power Pack.** I'm sure by now you've figured out what panties are her favorites, which ones make her feel a certain way and which ones you prefer. The objective now is for you to put together a "power pack" for her based on what her goals are for the week. It may be a red thong for Monday, a white bikini for Tuesday and a pair of blue booty shorts for Wednesday. You get the picture. The goal is that you create the power pack yourself by

going to the lingerie section and getting those skivvies. She will love this. If you want some extra brownie points, put together a Period Panty Power Pack, too. That'll really be a bonus.

3. **Show some extra affection.** It's always easy to want to hug your wife or girlfriend when you see *those* panties, but try to be a bit more affectionate even when you don't see them. It will show her that no matter what she is wearing, your affection remains constant. Trust me. There will be plenty of time for the touchy-feely panty moments.

Utilize the following pages to create your own action items from each chapter.

Bikini Day

Ladies

1. _____
   _____
   _____

2. _____
   _____
   _____

3. _____
   _____
   _____

Gentlemen

1. _____
   _____
   _____

2. _____
   _____
   _____

3. _____
   _____
   _____

Booty Shorts Anyone?

Ladies

1. _____
   _____
   _____

2. _____
   _____
   _____

3. _____
   _____
   _____

Gentlemen

1. _____
   _____
   _____

2. _____
   _____
   _____

3. _____
   _____
   _____

Thong Song

Ladies

1. _____
   _____
   _____

2. _____
   _____
   _____

3. _____
   _____
   _____

Gentlemen

1. _____
   _____
   _____

2. _____
   _____
   _____

3. _____
   _____
   _____

Granny Panties - Don't Be Fooled

Ladies

1. _____
   _____
   _____

2. _____
   _____
   _____

3. _____
   _____
   _____

Gentlemen

1. _____
   _____
   _____

2. _____
   _____
   _____

3. _____
   _____
   _____

Legally Commando

Ladies

1. _____
   _____
   _____

2. _____
   _____
   _____

3. _____
   _____
   _____

Gentlemen

1. _____
   _____
   _____

2. _____
   _____
   _____

3. _____
   _____
   _____

Period Panties - Embrace the Flow

Ladies

1. _____
   _____
   _____

2. _____
   _____
   _____

3. _____
   _____
   _____

Gentlemen

1. _____
   _____
   _____

2. _____
   _____
   _____

3. _____
   _____
   _____

Ain't Nothin' But a G-String

Ladies

1. _____
   _____
   _____

2. _____
   _____
   _____

3. _____
   _____
   _____

Gentlemen

1. _____
   _____
   _____

2. _____
   _____
   _____

3. _____
   _____
   _____

The End

Ladies

1. _____
   _____
   _____

2. _____
   _____
   _____

3. _____
   _____
   _____

Gentlemen

1. _____
   _____
   _____

2. _____
   _____
   _____

3. _____
   _____
   _____

Cheryl L. Smith Biography

Just shy of 19, life was amazing. Cheryl had married and brought to the world three beautiful children. Her marriage was wonderful, the family was perfect, and then the unthinkable happened. Her husband was diagnosed with cancer. Life suddenly stopped, but she never waivered. She took the bull by the horns, handling affairs at home and at the hospital too.

Her faith, love and proactive approach provided their family with another three years before her husband passed. Although the battle was grueling, this now 27 year old had found strength, perseverance and the ability to conquer any obstacle in a manner that many would have faltered beneath.

Over the next few years, and as a single parent, she returned to school acquiring a B.S. in Business Marketing and an M.B.A. She worked for the local newspaper successfully running an education program, then moved on to work for a regulatory agency while developing a non-profit organization focused on environmental education and then finally supporting the Department of Defense as a contractor for environmental management.

Today, Cheryl utilizes these years of experience in helping individuals and businesses get the results they desire, whether professionally or personally, through the art of successful communication.

To learn more about Cheryl and stay up to date with what's happening, follow her here:

Like Cheryl's Facebook page
https://www.facebook.com/CherylSmithEntrepreneur/

Follow her on Twitter
https://twitter.com/MsCherylLSmith

Check out her free resources
http://www.cheryllynnsmith.com/

Acknowledgments

To my family - Each and every one of you have been amazingly supportive of my decision to write this book. You've been in my corner from the start; rooting me on and listening to me share my experiences along the way. For that, I'm eternally grateful and blessed to have had you in my corner from the beginning and now to being a published author. Thank you.

To the Self-Publishing School community - You all have given me such guidance and confidence to keep pushing. You have held my hand and guided me through the enormous amount of questions I've had along the way. I could not have done this without your support and am eternally grateful. And finally, to my SPS accountability partner, Megan. I can't thank you enough for the brainstorming, knowledge and guidance through this process. This is just the beginning. We are on our way!

Credits:

Author Photos: Stephen Joseph Photography
Editing: Spencer Borup at Nerdy Wordsmith Ink

Love the book?
Tell your friends and leave a review!

Thank you so much for downloading my book. I am thrilled that you've chosen to become a part of the family. I do appreciate hearing all that you have to say and would greatly appreciate your feedback. Please leave an honest REVIEW on Amazon. Thanks so much!
Cheryl

Wonder HOW I wrote and published my own book?

NOW IT'S YOUR TURN

Discover the EXACT 3-step blueprint you need to become a bestselling author in 3 months.

Self-Publishing School helped me, and now I want them to help you with this FREE WEBINAR!

Even if you're busy, bad at writing, or don't know where to start, you CAN write a bestseller and build your best life.

With tools and experience across a variety niches and professions, Self-Publishing School is the only resource you need to take your book to the finish line!

DON'T WAIT

Watch this FREE WEBINAR now, and
Say "YES" to becoming a bestseller:
https://xe172.isrefer.com/go/curcust/cheryls

Made in the USA
Middletown, DE
22 May 2018